T0171559

Because
I Said So

Because
I Said So

And Other Tales from a
Less-Than-Perfect Parent

Dawn Meehan

HOWARD BOOKS
A DIVISION OF SIMON & SCHUSTER, INC.
New York · Nashville · London · Toronto · Sydney

Howard Books
A Division of Simon & Schuster, Inc.
1230 Avenue of the Americas
New York, NY 10020

First Howard Books trade paperback edition July 2011

HOWARD and colophon are trademarks of Simon & Schuster, Inc.

For information about special discounts for bulk purchases,
please contact Simon & Schuster Special Sales at 1-866-506-1949
or business@simonandschuster.com.

The Simon & Schuster Speakers Bureau can bring authors to
your live event. For more information or to book an event
contact the Simon & Schuster Speakers Bureau at 1-866-248-3049
or visit our website at www.simonspeakers.com.

Designed by Ruth Lee-Mui

Manufactured in the United States of America

1   3   5   7   9   10   8   6   4   2

Library of Congress Cataloging-in-Publication Data

Meehan, Dawn.
Because I said so : and other tales from a less-than-perfect parent / Dawn Meehan.
    p. cm.
1. Child rearing—Humor. 2. Parenting—Humor. I. Title.
    PN6231.C315M43 2011
    306.87402'07—dc22   2011016809

ISBN 978-1-4391-9176-7
ISBN 978-1-4516-1393-3 (ebook)

This book is dedicated to my readers. If it weren't for you, I wouldn't have a reason to stay at my computer writing all day and I'd have to get up and clean my house or get a real job or something. Thank you for giving me the excuse to not clean.

Contents

Things Happen for a Reason

I believe things happen for a reason.

For example, you slip and fall because the kids poured soap all over the kitchen floor. When you fall to the ground, you see your car keys, which have been missing for two days, shoved under the oven. If the kids hadn't poured soap on the floor, you wouldn't have fallen, and had you not fallen, it could've been years before you ever pulled the oven away from the wall to clean under it, thus finding your keys. It was meant to be.

Of course, if your kids hadn't shoved the keys under the oven in the first place, it wouldn't have happened to begin with, but that's a different story.

In March of 2006, I wrote a little story about how a baseball started a day of chaos with my kids. I used the story to sell the dirty old baseball on eBay. I don't know what possessed me to make an auction of it, but I did, and my auction attracted the attention of more than 220,000 people during the week it was for sale. I ended up selling the ball for $1,125 because people bid, not because they wanted the ball, but because my story had made them laugh! And best of all, I received e-mails from thousands of people telling me that the story made them feel a little better about their own parenting.

A year and a half after the baseball incident, I listed a pack of Pokémon cards on eBay, along with a humorous description of how these cards ended up in my cart while I was grocery shopping with my six children. I had just started a blog and I thought if people liked my eBay description, I could direct them to my blog. I wanted to share my stories with other parents out there in cyberspace and was hoping to make a little income from my blog as well. I had hopes of going from five hits a day on my blog to maybe fifty hits a day. What I got instead was 94,000 hits to my blog in one day. I thought the baseball auction had attracted attention, but this Pokémon card auction took off and spread through the Internet like a, well, like a virus. Long after the auction ended, people were forwarding the link to the auction and copying and pasting the shopping-trip description in e-mails to friends, family, and coworkers in all corners of the globe. Within a week of the auction's end, I'd received more than 10,000 e-mails from people around the world thanking me for the laugh, telling me what a great read my listing was, and asking me to write a book. I received all sorts of e-mail from people thanking me for helping them get through a bad day. People told me that I had somehow made a difference in their lives as they started to look at their kids with a little more humor. I slowly began to realize that my writing had touched some lives in a positive way.

Sometimes you have to be hit over the head before you figure out what you're supposed to do with your life. Sometimes, when you're a little dimwitted and don't get it the first time, God hits you over the head a second time and says, "Look, don't bury your talents. Use them." I believe these auctions were God's way of telling me to share my stories, to share about my own parenting struggles and failures in order to encourage parents everywhere.

I am a stay-at-home mom of six kids. People ask me all the time why I have six kids. I tell them the reason I have six is because I didn't want seven. My oldest son, Austin, is sixteen. He's smart as a whip, creative, artistic, and is starting to drive (heaven help me!). Next in line is Savannah, who is fourteen. Savannah is fun, easygoing, organized, and helps me more than she knows. Jackson is twelve years old and is followed by my daughter Lexington, who is nine. Jackson has an incredible memory. He's determined and compassionate, and like his mom, he loves to write. Lexi is my princess. She's a girly-girl who cares about everyone, and she has an awesome imagination. My seven-year-old son, Clayton, is extremely energetic, resourceful, and a little too smart for his own good, and my five-year-old daughter, Brooklyn, who is very much the baby of the family and used to being doted on and getting her way, brings up the rear. My children are the most wonderful, amazing blessings and give me immeasurable joy. They're also my greatest source of aggravation, and they make me question my sanity (and sometimes reach for the wine) every single day.

I was able to write this book because my kids have provided me with years of material. They've taught me so many things, like how a ringing phone releases a hormone in children that brings them running to you while speaking in their loudest voice, and that blue frosting will turn a toddler's poop neon green, and that oranges left rotting in a car in the sun leave a stench that could kill an elephant.

Of course, they've also taught me patience. They've taught me to look at the world through their eyes and appreciate all the little things they find fascinating. What is it that makes a glob of gum stuck to the sidewalk irresistible? Why is it that a butterfly must be chased and a flower must have every petal picked off and explored (and sometimes stuck up one's nose)? The world is absolutely fascinating when seen through little eyes.

They've taught me that I don't have a clue when it comes to parenting.

They've taught me unconditional love and sheer happiness. They've also taught me that I don't have a clue when it comes to parenting. Every time I think I have it figured out, they prove me wrong. Parenting is definitely a profession with on-the-job training. You learn as you go.

Most important, they've taught me if you're going to raise children, a sense of humor is an absolute must.

Chapter One

Baseball and Other Hazards
of Having Kids

Having children irreversibly changes your life. Before I had children, my husband and I talked about it. We discussed how we thought our lives would change with the arrival of a baby. We took classes on childbirth and parenting. We were prepared. Or so we thought.

The thing is, although we took classes and read books and knew what to expect as far as the baby's feeding, sleeping, diapering, and developmental milestones, we were clueless about all the other stuff that comes with having children. The kind of stuff that isn't covered in books.

For example, coming up with a name for your baby that you and your spouse both agree on is harder than you might think. And although you know your baby won't sleep through the night when it's first born, nothing really prepares you for the insomnia of mammoth proportions that you'll experience or the zombie-like state in which you will survive for months. Then there's the dreaded pregnancy weight gain and the subsequent attempts to lose the excess blubber.

When you're expecting your first child, no one tells you you'll soon be spending every second of your life in your car as you drive that child to baseball practice or gymnastics meets or swimming lessons. You don't really prepare for this ahead of time. One day you just find yourself in the position of chauffeur.

> Before you have children, you can't imagine yourself saying things like "Don't put chocolate milk in your pants," "Take the hot dog out of your nose," or "Because I said so!"

When you're pregnant, you don't realize that in about five years, you'll have to try out your acting skills by playing the part of the Tooth Fairy. This doesn't even cross your mind before you have kids. And you certainly can't imagine yourself saying things like "Don't put chocolate milk in your pants," "Take the hot dog out of your nose," or "Because I said so!"

Alas, these are just a few of the hazards of parenting.

A Rose by Any Other Name

My kids are all named after cities: Austin, Savannah, Jackson, Lexington, Clayton, and Brooklyn.

Yes, Clayton is actually a city, even though it doesn't sound like one. We were running out of good city names by the time we got to Clay, and we had a hard time deciding on a name. We didn't pick a name until the day after he was born, despite plenty of "helpful" suggestions from family and friends. Let's see if I can recall some of their wonderful name ideas. There was Schenectady, Tallahassee, Paul and Minnie (St. Paul and Minneapolis) if I had boy/girl twins, Albuquerque, Tuscaloosa, Kalamazoo, Chattanooga, Poughkeepsie, Punxsutawney, and, of course, my dad's favorite, Rancho Cucamonga.

As awesome as all these suggestions were, I figured I'd mess up my child enough on my own without giving him a name he'd never be able to spell. Can you imagine the therapy bill for a kid named Punxsutawney?

I didn't start out with the whole city theme on purpose. I just liked the names Austin and Savannah for my first two kids. After I had them, I realized they were both city names, and I decided to stick with the theme. It spiraled out of control from there. I continued it because I figured I couldn't have Austin, Savannah, Jackson, Lexington, and then Bob. It just wouldn't flow. So I gave each of my kids a city name.

With my fifth, Clayton, I'd narrowed down my choices to Dallas, Houston, Branson, and Clayton. (Yes, I used a copy of Rand McNally to get ideas.) My husband and I couldn't decide, so we let our other kids pick the baby's name from those four choices. Austin and Savannah both voted for Clayton. Jackson, on the other hand, opted to call him Slicker. He continued to call him Slicker for a good year. At least that was better than his original choice, Nemo.

My dad found all this amusing, and each time I gave birth to another grandchild, he was proud to stand up in church and say,

"I have a blessing to announce. My daughter has just given us another city!"

When I was pregnant with my sixth baby, a girl, I ran out of cities and had to move on to the boroughs. Thus Brooklyn was born.

I'm not sure why I bothered to give my kids names at all, because I never can remember them. I spit and sputter, going through a list of disjointed syllables.

> I'm not sure why I bothered to give my kids names at all, because I never can remember them.

"AusSavaJacksLexiBrook-Clayton, get over here right now!" You don't sound very authoritative when you can't remember your child's name. For some reason, the kids just don't take you seriously when you yell, "JacksSav, er, ClayLex, grrr, whatever your name is! You know who you are!"

My dad used to call my poor sister "Corky." Corky was the dog. We thought he was crazy. Now I know the truth: we made him crazy. I think I'll just start calling all my kids Larry to avoid confusion and mix-ups. "Hey Larry, come here." All the kids would come running. "Larry, set the table, please." The kids would all rush to place dishes on the table. Or, more likely, the kids would all look at me with blank stares, then nod knowingly to one another, confirming their beliefs that I'd officially lost my mind.

I think naming kids today is harder than in past generations. In the past, offspring were named after relatives. Names were chosen from a list of traditional names that had been used for generations. Nowadays, parents can name their children pretty much anything. When a parent names their child Kumquat, for example, society isn't shocked. Instead they nod and think, "Hmmm, Kumquat. That's got a nice ring to it." Traditional boys' names are given to girls. Girls' names are given to boys. Pet names are given to babies. Names of flowers, fruit, cars, and electronics are given to children. Miscellaneous combinations of letters are declared names and are bestowed upon daughters and sons. The funny thing is, the different, unique names parents come up with for their children are the very names that make it to the Top 100 list of names. Parents name their child Spleen or X or Zucchini, thinking that they'll be the only child with that name. But somehow the name catches on and there are four Spleens, Xs, or Zucchinis in your child's kindergarten class.

And then there's the most important part of naming your child: the nickname. My kids all have nicknames. All kids have nicknames, whether you want them to or not. You pore over baby-name books for nine months, agonizing over the all-important question of what you can name your baby so no one will give him a goofy nickname. It seems that for every choice you can think of, an unappealing nickname is just waiting to attach itself to your baby.

For example, maybe you like the name Joseph but detest the name Joey. No matter how hard you try, by the time the kid is in kindergarten, at least ten people will call him Joey. Let's say you're superadamant about calling your new baby son Joseph and you immediately correct anyone who utters Joe or Joey. He'll acquire a nickname like Skipper, Stinky, Rhino, or some equally ridiculous moniker that will stick with him for life. It just happens. You might as well accept it.

But the struggle for the right name is only the first of many hazards of having kids.

Sleeping Like a Baby

Sleeping like a baby. Now, tell me, who on earth came up with that nonsense? Talk about an oxymoron. I haven't had a full night's sleep in sixteen years!

The minute you see that positive pregnancy test, you can pretty much give up on a good night's sleep for the rest of your life. Sleep deprivation is a way of life for parents. I'm saying that sleep deprivation is a way of life for *parents* instead of *moms* because I don't want to leave out the one father in Passaic, New Jersey, who actually gets up with his baby. For the rest of you moms who walk around like zombies all day because you've had only thirty-five minutes of sleep, you are not alone. Why do you think Starbucks is so popular?

It all starts in pregnancy. Some say the sleeplessness of pregnancy is just the body's way of preparing us for the sleepless nights that lie ahead once the baby arrives. I say it's a cruel joke designed to make us question our decision to have a child.

For anyone who has never been pregnant and can't understand how pregnancy could cause difficulty sleeping, try this: eat your weight in salt and walk twenty miles. That should sufficiently swell your ankles. Next, eat fifteen extrahot burritos to make sure you get a whopping case of heartburn. Then do a little weight-lifting. A dead lift of five hundred pounds should do the trick to make your back feel almost as bad as a pregnant woman's. Before retiring for the night, drink a fifty-five-gallon drum of water to ensure you'll have to get up to pee every five minutes all night long. Finally, as you lie down to sleep, put a twenty-pound watermelon on your stomach. Sweet dreams!

After the baby is born, when the physical discomforts of pregnancy are gone, you still don't get a full night's sleep. You know the baby will wake up during the night. After all, you took the classes. You know the drill. You were warned that your precious newborn would wake up to eat in her first few weeks of life, but nothing really prepares you for the sleep loss that new moms experience. Imagine a smoke alarm that goes off two inches from your head in the middle of the night. The only way to turn off the incessant wailing is to carry it around with you for an hour.

Nothing really prepares you for the sleep loss that new moms experience.

I'm sorry to say that it doesn't get much better as the kids get older. Instead of getting up to eat, they get up because it's storming or because they've had bad dreams or because they need to tell you something they forgot to tell you five hours earlier when everyone was awake.

When older kids get up in the middle of the night, they don't scream and cry. You think that would be a plus, don't you? It isn't. What older kids do is walk into your bedroom, stand with their face a mere inch away from yours, and then stare at you until somewhere, in the deep recesses of your sleeping brain, you sense them there and crack open your eyelids to a pair of giant eyeballs staring at you. This scares the living daylights out of you, and you will not be able to get back to sleep for at least an hour and probably only with the aid of some nitroglycerin pills.

Then there are the kids who like to stall when it's time to go to bed. Every night, it's the same routine. "Can I have a drink of water? Will you read me one more story? I have to go to the bathroom. Can I have another glass of water? Mom, where do monkeys sleep? Can I have another glass of water? Can you help me find my teddy bear? Why does the sun go down at night? Can I have a snack? I have to go to the bathroom again. How old are you, Mom? Can I have another glass of water? Why do you look so tired, Mom?"

Perhaps you'll be blessed with children who sleep through the night and don't give you too much grief about going to bed. Even still, once you become a mom, you probably won't get a full eight hours of sleep on a regular basis. When your child is a baby, you'll lie awake gazing at their perfect little faces. You'll periodically lay your hand on their chest, checking for the reassuring rise and fall of their breathing. You'll worry about your child's health and whether her growth will be stunted if she lives on ketchup and M&M's for a month. You'll worry about his social development: will he be an outcast forever because he bit another kid at preschool? As they grow older, your worries will change: am I really ruining my daughter's life by not buying her a cell phone; they'd better be home by curfew; I hope they make wise choices; I pray they don't get in a car accident—but you'll still lie awake and worry about them.

With all that extra awake time, you could do something productive such as scrub your floors, pay bills, or catch up on reading. I personally like to watch my children sleep, however. They look so angelic when they're sleeping. Somehow those kids who were running around like rabid hyenas just an hour ago now look so peaceful, so sweet that I forget how they were flinging pudding

at the ceiling after dinner. When they're asleep, I can easily remember why I love this job.

What Does the Tooth Fairy Do
with All Those Teeth?

Of course, there will be plenty of other things you'll be doing instead of sleeping. Moms are always the ones to stay up late to finish chores. Funny how that works. When Dad says he's going to
bed, he actually goes to bed. When Mom says she's going to bed,
what she really means is that she's going to wash some bottles,
fold a load of laundry, check homework, fill out permission slips,
feed the dog, make the school lunches, lay out clothes for the
little ones, and write notes and lists of chores she will need to
accomplish tomorrow. But sometimes Mom gets to do something
fun, too.

Playing Tooth Fairy is something I never thought much about
until my first child lost his first tooth. He literally lost it. It fell
out on the playground amid four thousand bushels of wood chips.
What did I do? What any normal mother would have done. I
got down on my hands and knees and searched the wood chips
around the swings for five hours. Okay, so maybe it wasn't really
five hours, but it felt like it. Those wood chips are sharp on the
knees!

I really can't complain, because my mother searched through
much, much worse when I was a child. When I was in grade
school, I accidentally threw my retainer into the trash compac-
tor with the rest of my garbage at lunchtime. That little piece
of plastic probably cost a thousand dollars, so of course my mom
went back to the school cafeteria and waded through piles of

garbage looking for it. As a special bonus for my mom, they had served turkey, mashed potatoes, gravy, and cranberry sauce for lunch. Can you believe she actually found it? I'm sure I didn't appreciate it at the time, but now as a mom myself, I can't believe she went to those lengths to find the retainer. There is no way my stomach would've been able to handle the joy of searching through mountains of mashed potatoes, gravy, and cranberry sauce. If it had happened to me, my kid would have grown up with crooked teeth.

Back to my son's lost tooth. Of course, I didn't find his tiny little tooth anywhere. What was I thinking? In fact, I think the saying *needle in a haystack* should be replaced with *tooth in a woodchip pile*. I came up with the brilliant idea of having him draw a picture of his lost tooth so the Tooth Fairy would know that he'd really lost his first baby tooth. I told him she would understand and everything would be fine. It worked that time, but apparently the Tooth Fairy is a bit forgetful. Sometimes (yes, it's happened more than once) the Tooth Fairy fails to make an appearance.

> I was convinced the only thing he would remember from his childhood is that the Tooth Fairy forgot him.

Is there a more heartbreaking sight than your child walking into your bedroom first thing in the morning, holding the lost tooth and saying, "The Tooth Fairy forgot me last night"?

The first time this happened at my house, I felt absolutely horrible. I knew I totally deserved the Worst Mother of the Year award. Looking into Austin's tear-filled eyes, I started to cry, too. How could I have forgotten? I worried that I'd screwed up my child for life. I was convinced the only thing he would remember from his childhood is that the Tooth Fairy forgot him. I ~~quickly made excuses~~ came up with a plausible explanation. Obviously the Tooth Fairy was extremely busy last night. Many kids must have lost teeth yesterday. Yeah, that's it! I'm sure she'll come tonight. I'm positive. Just put your tooth back under your pillow again tonight, sweetheart.

Then the Tooth Fairy took out a second mortgage on her house so she could leave a big guilt offering under my child's pillow.

When my daughter lost her tooth on Christmas Eve one year, the Tooth Fairy forgot to make an appearance again. On Christmas morning, when my daughter told me sadly that the Tooth Fairy hadn't come, I said, "That's because the air traffic controllers in Fairyland had a problem. The Tooth Fairy and Santa Claus couldn't share airspace. I'm sure she'll come by tonight when Santa's not flying around."

My kids, creative children that they are, once made up a questionnaire for the Tooth Fairy. "What is your real name? Do you have a pet? What do you do with the teeth? Is there more than one Tooth Fairy? Where do you live? What's your favorite food?" It went on and on and on. When my daughter lost a tooth, she left this questionnaire along with her tooth. Did she leave the questionnaire under her pillow? At the foot of her bed? Nooooo, that would be too easy. She stuck it on her wall with a thumbtack. Not just any wall—the wall on the far side of her bed.

Now, my daughter sleeps in a loft bed. You should've seen me climbing up her ladder and attempting to maneuver in ways a human should never move, trying to get this piece of paper off the wall. I'm a short person, so I had to lean on the bed as

I reached across my innocently sleeping daughter. As I braced myself by leaning on her bed, my weight pushing on her pillow made her roll toward me at the side of her bed. I backed off so she wouldn't fall out of bed. As I carefully scooted her back toward the wall, she turned over but didn't wake up. So far, so good.

I made a brave second attempt at the paper. Yes! I managed to rip the thing from the wall, but the thumbtack went flying! I couldn't see it in the dim light, and I was afraid that my daughter would roll over it in her sleep and get hurt. So there I was, still balancing on her ladder, leaning over her bed, searching in the dark for a thumbtack.

A stabbing pain in my hand told me that I'd discovered it. However, my little yelp awakened my daughter, so I leapt (okay, more like stumbled) from the ladder and hit the deck. There I was, on the floor, holding perfectly still and trying not to breathe. After what seemed like two and a half days, I could hear her deep, even breathing, but not wanting to chance waking her or her sister, who was sleeping on the other side of the room, I did the army crawl on my elbows and stomach across her floor and out the door. Whew! The lengths we go to so we can preserve the innocence of childhood. That sacrifice alone should cancel out the whole forgetting about the tooth thing, right?

That was the easy part. After that I had to come up with answers to a dozen questions.

"What is your real name?"

Hmmm, what is my real name? What is my real name? What would be a good Tooth Fairy name? Toothy? Nah. Incisor? Nope. Bicuspid? I don't think so. Mary? Too ordinary. Crystal? Hmmm . . . maybe. That sounds like it could be the name of a fairy.

Okay, next. "Where do you live?"

Ugh. Toothtropolis? No good. Toothtown? Blech. In a castle in the sky? Well, that sounds kind of fairylike.

"What do you do with the teeth?"

What do I do with the teeth? Oh for Pete's sake! I don't know! How did she come up with these questions?

"Do you have any pets?"

Would the Tooth Fairy have any pets? What kind of pet would the Tooth Fairy have? A pet with a lot of teeth? How about an alligator?

Halfway through the questionnaire, I realized I was going to have to put this thing back up in her room. I decided it was time to call in reinforcements. I woke my then husband (who has monkey-long arms) and briefed him on his mission. "You have to put the paper back on her wall and leave it without waking her." He accepted his mission.

The next morning, my daughter told me, "I saw Daddy putting the paper on the wall last night." I started to freak out. He blew it! After all that, he blew it! Just goes to show, if you want a job done right, you need to do it yourself!

Then, my daughter continued with, "I guess he wanted to read what the Tooth Fairy wrote." I tried to suppress a smile. She was none the wiser, at least for a little while longer.

Put Me in, Coach

Playing Tooth Fairy is actually tame compared to playing coach or cheerleader for your child's sporting events. No one told me that as a parent, I would no longer have hobbies of my own. Too late I realized that all of my free time was suddenly devoted to attending my kids' activities.

Kids today are busy. They're involved with sports, clubs, after-school activities, volunteer work, church, Scouts, lessons, classes. Basically, this means parents have to take out a large loan to finance said activities. It also means parents spend a minimum of forty hours per week driving their children here and there.

For your child to participate in an average dance class, you have to pay for three semesters of classes, a leotard, tights that you need to replace every week when your daughter gets a run in them, and ballet shoes that she outgrows every other month. At the end of the three semesters, you need to purchase tickets to see your own child in her dance recital. Of course, if you love your child, you'll also purchase the professional pictures of her in her costume and the professionally produced DVD of her recital. If your child takes tap dance in addition to ballet, you can double those costs. If you have two children in dance, quadruple them.

> If you love your child, you'll purchase the professional pictures of her in her costume and the professionally produced DVD of her recital.

If your kids play baseball, you have to pay not only for the fees to sign them up to play in the league but also for a helmet, bat, glove, uniform, water bottle, bat bag, professional pictures, and, of course, the ER bill when they're hit in the mouth with a 60 mph fastball.

Now imagine having six kids who are involved in Boy Scouts, Cub Scouts, Girl Scouts, Brownies, baseball, T-ball, softball, ballet, tap, jazz, piano lessons, saxophone lessons, clarinet lessons, basketball, volleyball, art club, jazz band, French club, church youth group, and cross-country. To finance this, you have to make some adjustments. Giving up extras such as movies, vacations, clothes, and food should free up some of the necessary income. You will also have to sell your house, which is really not a big deal since you'll be spending every waking moment in your car anyway.

I probably spend about half my life each spring watching baseball games. I don't mind too much. Baseball season means it's time to kick back in the bleachers with a hot dog and a cold drink. Time to hang out with friends and work on your tan while cheering the home team on to victory. Unless, of course you're talking about your kids' baseball season. That's a whole other ball game.

First off, we live in Illinois, where we don't have spring. We have two seasons: winter and construction. Winter lasts through the middle of May and then construction season starts. We go from negative 50 degrees and snow to 190 overnight. When baseball season starts in April, we have to wear winter coats, gloves, and hats to the games. We bring thermoses of hot chocolate and wrap up in blankets as we huddle together, watching the kids play. Then, come May fifteenth, we strip off our parkas, replacing them with tank tops and shorts. We replace the thermoses of hot chocolate with icy lemonade and the hand warmers with sunscreen.

When baseball season ends, I miss the fun of watching my kids play. I miss spending time as a family at the ballpark. I miss seeing my kids make amazing catches, painful-looking slides into home plate, and awesome throws to first for the out.

What I don't miss is trying to get dinner on the table at four so we can be at a field across town by five. I definitely don't miss trying to get the kids to finish their homework the minute they walk in the door from school. I don't miss packing up coolers with water and bags with jackets, sunscreen, toys, coloring books, and snacks for the little ones. I don't miss the endless questions: "Do you have your bat? Do you have your glove? Why isn't your glove in your bag? Where's your bag? Well, go get it. Yes, now. Do you have your cup on? Well, you might want to consider putting it on. No, I don't have it; I'm not in charge of it. We have to leave in a minute. Find your stuff and get it in the car!" I don't miss repeatedly pulling Brooklyn down from the bleachers on which she's been climbing or chasing Clay away from a busy street while trying to watch the game. And I especially don't miss the planning and coordination it takes to get six kids to games and activities on opposite sides of town at the same time.

In baseball season, I use a huge color-coded calendar the size of my refrigerator to coordinate games, fields, and times. I used to complain about how tough it was for my husband and me to get everyone where they needed to be on time. Little did I know that that would be a piece of cake compared to doing it all on my own. As a single mom whose ex-husband isn't involved in the kids' lives, I've had to get creative in respect to getting my children where they need to be. I threw a challenge out to my children the other day: "The first person to build a working teleportation device gets out of doing chores for the rest of their life. Have at it!" I found my six-year-old, Clay, walking to his bedroom with the toaster, a shoelace, a cup full of grass clippings, and my deodorant. I think he's onto something.

I love watching the little kids play, though. If you've never been to a Little League game, you're missing out. When at bat, kids will take a minimum of fifty-two swings before getting a hit.

When they actually make contact with the ball, they stand there in shock for a full minute, and then they turn to their parents in the stands, faces beaming, and shout, "Did you see that? I hit the ball!" You smile back, beaming with pride, video camera rolling, while frantically waving your arms in the sky like an air traffic controller landing a plane, and scream, "RUN!!!!" However, there's really no reason for the child to run as fast as his little legs will carry him, because the first baseman is busy looking at a butterfly and hasn't even noticed that someone hit the ball. Meanwhile, the third baseman is building a sandcastle over the plate and the pitcher is walking to the dugout because he has to go potty.

Your child finally starts to run the bases. The only problem is, instead of running to first, he runs to third and keeps going. The shortstop somehow manages to scoop up the ball and starts chasing after your son, who is now rounding second, continuing his backward trot around the bases. The shortstop continues to chase him in a makeshift game of tag until they both hit home plate and fall over laughing. This is pretty much how five-year-old children play baseball.

The older kids are also fun to watch. Cheering for your child's team is exciting. I love watching amazing plays and really close games. It's great entertainment unless it's your child on the line. For example, I remember one of my daughter's games last year. We were up by one. It was the bottom of the last inning, and the other team was up to bat. The tying run was on third and bases were loaded. They had two outs. The girl up to bat had a full count. Not too much pressure, right?

She struck out. Although I feel awful for any kid stuck in that position, I was secretly thanking God that it wasn't my daughter who got the last out. I can only imagine, twenty years from now, one of my kids mumbling to their psychiatrist, "If only I'd hit that ball back when I was ten years old . . ."

I don't usually get to see much of the game because I'm busy chasing my other kids around. Once while I was trying to watch the game, I noticed that Clay was chewing something.

"What do you have in your mouth?" I demanded.

"Nothing," he replied.

Prying his mouth open, I saw that he was chewing gum. Where did he get gum? I quickly realized that he had picked it off the bottom of the bleachers, of course.

Do you know what's on the underside of the bleachers at any given ballpark? I'm not sure, but it all found its way into his mouth that day. Mmmm, nothing like month-old, already chewed gum covered in dirt and bugs. Ewww! As I forced him to spit out the nasty gum (into my outstretched hand, naturally), I heard the coach shout, "Hang on! There's a little kid on the field!" I looked up to see that the baby had escaped her stroller and had toddled onto the field, heading for first base. "Put me in, coach!"

Arghhh! Is baseball season over yet?

Diet Starts Monday. Again.

Another hazard of having children is the dreaded weight gain. They say you put on an extra ten pounds per child. I've had six. Do the math.

If you're one of those skinny "I only gained seven pounds when I was pregnant and then I dropped down to a size two after I had the baby" moms, put down this book, go make yourself an ice cream sundae, and don't come back to finish reading this until you've packed on at least twenty pounds.

Are the skinny ones gone? Good. Okay, for the rest of us who are carrying around a little extra baby weight despite the fact that our "babies" are now in high school, here's the secret to losing weight . . .

Are you kidding? Do you think I know the secret to losing weight? If I did, this would be a book on weight loss, and it definitely isn't.

I think I know the secret to gaining weight, though. First, sample everything you cook all day. Finish the food left on your kids' plates. (You can't waste it; you spent good money on that food and besides, there are starving kids in Africa.) Buy fat-laden snacks "for the kids" and then sneak some yourself. Go all day without eating because you're too busy and then inhale everything in sight at dinnertime. (That does wonders for your metabolism too, by the way.) And finally, make sure the only exercise you have time for is bending over to pick up toys and wrestling your children into their car seats. That ought to do the trick.

I recently got on the scale for the first time in a month and came to the shocking realization that I'd gained slightly less than a metric ton. I have no idea how this happened. I mean, my diet is exemplary. Today, for example, I had two cups of cream with a little coffee for flavor and a doughnut, which was stale, so I'm pretty sure it doesn't count. At church, we celebrated a birthday with cake after the worship service. I think the cake was blessed, and holy cake can't have many calories. Of course I had to finish my son's slice, as well: waste not, want not. For lunch I had a peanut butter sandwich, about seventy pretzels (but they were the little skinny stick kind so they don't count) and half my weight in chocolate. The chocolate didn't even taste very good, and if you don't enjoy the food you're eating, you don't have to count those calories. I had a big, fat cheeseburger for dinner, along with enough fries to keep Idaho in business, but I ate that while standing up and doing dishes because I was in a hurry to leave and play chauffeur to my daughter, and everyone knows that food consumed while standing doesn't count. Plus, I washed it all down with a Diet Coke, which negates the calories in the cheeseburger, so really I think I should be losing weight.

Thinking that maybe the whole diet thing wasn't going to do the trick, I decided to try to add a little exercise to my days. My kids talked me into trying their Dance Dance Revolution. "It's a great workout, Mom," they insisted.

If you're unfamiliar with this, I'll explain. It's a mat, divided into nine sections that you place on the floor and plug into a video game console. The video game shows arrows that scroll across the screen at the speed of light. You're supposed to see these arrows and your brain is supposed to make the connection of where your feet are supposed to go. "There's an arrow pointing to the left, so I need to step to the left. There's an arrow pointing up, so I need to move my foot up." That is what is *supposed* to happen. What happened in reality was that these arrows flashed across the screen at an alarmingly fast rate. My brain got all confused and I started stomping around on the mat like an Irish dancer wearing hiking boots while flailing her arms around wildly swatting at an imaginary swarm of bees. I ended in a sweating, tangled knot, while my kids—who were watching me—doubled over and fell off the couch laughing.

Realizing that Dance Dance Revolution was not for me, I borrowed my parents Gazelle. I highly recommend this. I used this almost every day. It really made quite a nice clothes hanger. I tried to do the Buns of Steel video, but quickly realized that it wasn't intended for people who have buns of pudding. I tried Tae Bo, but accidentally hit myself in the face, causing a black eye. Actually, doing those workout videos just made me bitter and angry. I mean, there were these skinny models working out, looking perfectly coiffed and made up, not a drop of sweat on them. Their perfectly smooth skin glowed, they had cute little workout outfits, and huge smiles plastered on their faces as if to convince me that they were enjoying every minute of exercise. I, on the other hand, had no makeup, my hair was in a ponytail, and I was wearing ill-fitting pants, a sweat-drenched T-shirt, and an angry frown. Watching supermodels work out on my screen was definitely not the way to go.

> I tried to do the Buns of Steel video, but I quickly realized that it wasn't intended for people who have buns of pudding.

So I paid a membership fee to join my local gym. I kept meaning to actually go there and do a little exercise, but I don't like to jump into these things. After a few months passed, I decided to make use of my membership before it expired, so I met my friend at the gym. My plan was to walk around the indoor track for two hours.

What on earth was I thinking??? TWO hours?! The most strenuous thing I've done in the past eight years is blow my nose. I admit that after I had my third baby, I started doing step aerobics five times a week. I lost a ton of weight, I looked good, and I felt great. In fact, I turned into one of those sickening people who actually *liked* to exercise. I looked forward to my workout and felt sad if I missed it. Luckily, I got over that.

When I joined the gym this time, I was once again struggling to add exercise to my daily routine of cleaning spilled milk off the kitchen floor, changing toxic diapers, fishing the ice pack out of the toilet (don't ask), and trying to get marker stains out of clothes.

So I got up the energy to meet my friend at the walking track. I arrived at the gym and drove around for half an hour looking for the closest parking place, because why should I get exercise by walking from my car to the door when I could give the gym all my money to let me walk around inside their building?

What I didn't realize was that when my friend said, "Let's walk," she really meant, "Let's run as if we're being chased by chainsaw-wielding madmen."

Oh. My. Gosh.

So there we are at the gym. She's running along, not even breaking a sweat, and there I am with my stubby little legs working double time to catch up to my friend, who is approximately seventeen feet tall. I'm lumbering along, looking like the full-grown mountain troll in the Harry Potter movie, drool forming at the corner of my mouth, sweat pouring down my face, my legs protesting the cruel and unusual punishment.

And my friend was not only running but also *talking*! I wasn't even able to gulp enough oxygen to support breathing, let alone *talking*. She's easily conversing about this and that, and I'm making little guttural grunts in response. Somewhere around the four hundredth lap, I had a heart attack. Who ever said that exercise was good for you?!

Oh well, I guess the diet starts again Monday. On the menu

is water for breakfast, lettuce for lunch, and a Tic Tac for dinner. Now I'm off to search for a snack. I've already looked in my fridge twice, but perhaps the food fairies came and left something good to snack on while I was writing this. Hey, it's not Monday yet.

Why Is My Mother's Voice Coming out of My Mouth?

No one warned me about what is probably the most horrifying hazard of parenting. It's happened slowly, a little bit at a time, so I didn't even notice for a long time. Then, recently, it hit me.

I'm turning into my mother.

I refuse to say that I've turned into her, as that implies there's no turning back. I haven't completely turned into her, but I'm well on my way.

The other day, I heard my mother's voice come out of my mouth as I told my son, "You can't go to school wearing that. Do you know it might not even hit thirty degrees outside today? I was watching the news last night and the weatherman said it was going to be really cold. He said there was going to be a high of only thirty-four degrees. There's also an eighty-five percent chance of snow this afternoon. By the time you get out of school, the roads will be terrible. I hope they have trucks out salting right now. They're saying it's going to be one of the worst snowstorms of the century. I need to run to the store first thing this morning and get supplies. We might be stuck inside for several days until they can plow the roads. You need to put a scarf and gloves on before you leave for school. Oh, and boots! Wear your boots. You don't want to walk home in four feet of snow without your boots."

My son stared at me, mouth agape. "Since when did you start worrying about the weather? You sound like Yia Yia." (My kids call my mom YiaYia, which is grandmother in Greek.)

My son was right. I never used to care about the weather. I used to scoff when my mother would call me *on* the phone to warn me to get *off* the phone because of thunderstorms and lightning. I used to roll my eyes when she'd tell me a blizzard was coming and I'd better get to the grocery store and make sure we had milk and diapers on hand. I would laugh when she'd suggest I stay home instead of driving to a meeting in the rain and fog. Yet here I was, worrying about a possible snowstorm—even making plans to go to the store and stock up just in case! And when did I start watching the news just to get a glimpse of the weather forecast, anyway?

Worrying about the weather is not the only reason I fear I'm turning into my mother. The other day I drove two miles out of my way to avoid making a left turn across traffic while running errands. When did this happen? I never used to be afraid of traffic, left turns, or merging onto the expressway. And it gets worse. On more than one occasion, I've involuntarily thrown my right arm out across the passenger in my car as I stopped quickly. Really, do I think that my outstretched arm will be enough to keep my passenger from flying out the window? Why do moms do this? Is it a natural instinct? At what point in your life does this wild arm flinging start to happen, and more important, is there a way to stop it?

A few weeks ago I found myself complaining that my kids used too much toilet paper. I started ranting about paper waste and devised a toilet-paper rationing system in my head, allotting each individual six squares per use. I was thankfully able to quash that one before the words came out of my mouth.

I've definitely developed my mom's supersonic sense of hearing. From across the house, behind a closed door, I can hear my kids plotting and planning. "Just shove your clothes under the bed and don't tell Mom. Shhhh," sounds like a shout in my mom ears. Not only can I hear whispers from my kids, but my ears seem to be sensitive to other noises as well. More often than I'd like to admit, I walk into the family room and tell my kids, "Turn the TV down! Why is it so loud?" My mom was forever telling me to turn down the volume when I was a kid. I couldn't understand what was wrong with her ears at the time; now I can't understand what's wrong with my kids' ears. Why do they need to have the TV blaring away? Maybe all this loud music and television has permanently damaged their little eardrums. That would explain why I have to repeat myself multiple times before they hear what I'm saying.

When I recognized what all the signs meant, I called my sister in a panic.

"Deb!" I gasped. "Help me! I think I'm turning into Mom."

"Yeah, I know." She was so matter-of-fact.

"You know?" I was incredulous. Maybe it was too late for me. Other people were already noticing.

"When did this happen?" I asked.

"About the time you started having kids," she replied.

"For sixteen years?!" I sat down, deflated. I guess it's inevitable. You have kids, and you turn into your parents.

"I think it's pretty funny. Remember last week at church? You pulled an old tissue out of your pocket, and wiped your son's

I guess it's inevitable. You have kids, and you turn into your parents.

25

face with it. And last month when you were at our house for the birthday party, you licked your finger and used it to wipe frosting off your daughter's face."

I didn't think it was so funny.

"At least you're not scared of roller coasters and carnival rides like Mom," my sister assured me.

I remembered the last time I was at an amusement park with my family. You couldn't have paid me to ride those roller coasters, but there was no way I was letting my sister know of yet another way I was turning into Mom. When did roller coasters stop being thrilling and start being scary? When did I start envisioning the cars breaking loose from the track and crashing to the ground hundreds of feet below? Instead of anxiously waiting in line for my turn on the tallest ride, I recalled newspaper stories of horrible malfunctions on amusement park rides.

My sister was just getting started. "You are totally like Mom! You're always making lists just like she does. I bet you even have a list to keep track of all your lists!"

It's true. I don't trust myself to remember anything. I make lists for the grocery store. I make lists of meals I'm planning for the week. I make lists of phone calls I need to make. I make lists of jobs I want to accomplish around the house. In fact, sometimes I add a job I've already completed so I can cross it off the list and feel like I've accomplished something. I make lists of Christmas presents I need to get for my family. I make lists of presents I've already bought. I make guest lists for birthday parties and lists of who's bringing what dish to potluck cookouts. I make lists of clothing I need to pack when we go camping. I make lists of things I need to do around the house before leaving on vacation. You'd think I do nothing all day but make lists!

I hung up with my sister, feeling a little depressed. My daughter walked by and said, "You're finally off the phone! You talk as much as YiaYia does." I remembered my mom spending a lot of time on the phone talking with friends when I was a kid. I wondered how any person could talk so much. Now I know. We talk on the phone to bring a little sanity into our lives. It's tough going all day without speaking to another adult.

I sat there thinking of all the traits I'd inherited from my mother and wanted to cry, but then I remembered how my mom used to sew homemade Halloween costumes for my sister and me. She made a home-cooked dinner, complete with sides and dessert that we ate together as a family every night, and there were almost always freshly baked cookies to enjoy after school.

My mother was always excited during the holidays. She used to wake us up early on New Year's Day so we could watch the parades. She'd bring in the TV trays and make a yummy brunch for us to enjoy in the family room—what a treat! Every Easter she'd take us shopping for a new dress, shoes (black, of course because it wasn't Memorial Day yet) and matching bonnets, gloves, and purses.

We always brought out the boxes of Christmas decorations the day after Thanksgiving. My dad would put together the artificial tree and string a million lights on it while my sister, mother, and I placed the decorations around the house in the same spots year after year. When the tree was all lighted, my mom poured everyone a glass of eggnog, and my sister and I hung our ornaments on the tree while listening to records of Christmas music on the stereo.

My mom used to have my sister and me sit on her lap while she read stories to us, and she'd tuck us in every night.

Hmmm . . . remembering all the wonderful momlike things she's done over the years, I find myself wishing I was just a little bit more like her. I guess it wouldn't be such a bad thing to turn into my mom, after all.

Chapter Two

Shopping with Kids: The Final Frontier

Before I had kids, I thought, *How hard could it be to go shopping with a child?* What is the big deal? I've since learned that shopping with kids is ~~a horrifying experience~~ an adventure. You never know what might happen while you're out in public with your kids, but it almost always includes moments that either embarrass you or make you want to run screaming from the store. Taking children shopping is also a learning experience.

My own children have taught me many things, like the fact that toddlers can and will escape from any shopping cart or stroller you try to strap them in, so it's best to use a five-point harness and duct tape. They've also generously taught me that if you dare to try on clothes while shopping with your children, you should be prepared to run out of the fitting room half naked to chase down an escaped toddler wreaking havoc in the clothes racks. I've learned that if you hear the phrase "Cleanup on aisle fifteen," there's a pretty good chance you'll find *your* child in aisle fifteen.

However, shopping with kids can be less painful than getting a root canal without Novocain if you use some common sense and keep some basic guidelines in mind. For example, to avoid an excursion of disastrous proportions, do not schedule shopping around nap and meal times, which leaves you basically from 9:00 a.m. to 9:15 a.m. It's hard enough to get your shopping done without a cranky toddler who needs sleep or food. Cranky, hungry children are no fun to shop with, especially if you're hungry and tired, too. If you know you're going to be gone for more than a few minutes, bring along a couple of toys and some snacks to occupy the kids. And don't forget extra diapers and wipes. Murphy's Law dictates that even if you're just running out to the library, your child will fill his diaper while you're there.

Before shopping with the kids, make a list of items you need and stick to it. Of course, if you find something else you simply must have, just add it to your list and then you can buy it guilt-free. When shopping with your children, allow about eight times the amount of time it would take you to shop by yourself. Expect to make at least seventeen impromptu trips to the bathroom and stops at restaurants and gas stations for drinks. Keep in mind your children's limits. If you're going to shop for clothing for yourself and will need to try on multiple items, you'll be better off if you can find someone to leave the kiddos with, unless you're a total glutton for punishment.

Most important, remember to laugh. Try to see shopping through their eyes. Little kids are amazed by the things we take for granted. When was the last time you marveled at the flower display at your local grocery store? Have you ever walked around the store with your head tilted back, admiring how high the ceilings are? And I bet it's been a while since you tried to lick the bars of the shopping cart just to see what they taste like. Take time to look around and talk to your

> *When shopping with your children, allow about eight times the amount of time it would take you to shop by yourself.*

children about the sights and sounds at the store. Play games and laugh with them. Believe me, this will make any shopping trip much more bearable. You may even find that it's enjoyable. Well, more enjoyable than poking yourself in the eye with a sharp stick, anyway.

Adventures in Grocery Shopping

You haven't lived until you've gone grocery shopping with six kids in tow. I would rather swim, covered in bait, through the English Channel, be a contestant on *Fear Factor* when they're having pig brains for lunch, or do fourth-grade math than take my six kids to the grocery store. Because I absolutely detest grocery shopping, I tend to put it off as long as possible. There comes a time, however, when I'm peering into the fridge and thinking, *Hmmm, what can I make with ketchup, Italian dressing, and half an onion,* that I decide I can't avoid going to the grocery store any longer. Before beginning this most treacherous mission, I gather all the kids together and give them the Lecture.

The Lecture goes like this: "We have to go to the grocery

store. Now here are the rules: do not ask me for anything, do not poke the packages of meat in the butcher section, do not test the laws of physics by trying to take out the bottom can in the pyramid-shaped display, do not play baseball with oranges in the produce section, and most important, do not try to leave your brother at the store again."

I'm sad to say that this has actually happened. One time while I was shopping at Target with my then five children, I was trying to check out and pay for my merchandise when Jackson asked me if he could walk over a couple of aisles to look at Pokémon cards. I was putting my merchandise on the conveyor belt and making sure I'd picked up everything on my list, so I nodded distractedly to Jackson, who took off to aisle thirteen.

After paying for my items, I maneuvered the cart around the million people who are always at Target on a Saturday and started walking to the car, which was parked four and a half miles away because, again, it was a Saturday at Target. At the car, I looked around and did a head count. One, two, three, four, four, four . . . where's five? *Who's* five? Who's missing???

Eventually I figured out Jackson was missing.

"Where's Jackson?" I asked. "Was he with us in the parking lot?"

The kids all calmly answered, "No, he's still inside looking at Pokémon cards."

"You *knew* this and didn't tell me? Why didn't you tell me we were leaving him behind?" I demanded.

"He bugs us," they said, shrugging. "Can't we just leave him here?"

Ah, the bonds between siblings.

Anyway, once the kids have been briefed about the rules, it's time to go. When we reach the store, I drive around the parking lot looking for a space next to a cart return. Other people avoid these spaces, but I search for them. I don't care about the possibility of dents and scratches on my minivan; I just know how much time it takes to return a cart to a corral that's twelve rows over, and leaving the kids alone in the car that long is not wise. I'll return to see that three-quarters of the groceries have been opened, spilled, and/or eaten, so I risk the dents from runaway carts and park next to the cart return.

We always grab not one but two shopping carts. I wear the baby in a sling, the two little children sit in the carts, my middle son walks, and I push one cart while my oldest son pushes the other one. My oldest daughter is not allowed to push a cart. Ever. Why? Because the last time I let her push the cart, she smashed into my ankles so many times my feet had to be amputated by the end of our shopping trip. This is not a good thing. You try running after a toddler with no feet sometime.

At this point, someone generally looks at our two carts and asks me, "Are they all yours?" I answer good-naturedly, "Yep!"

"Oh my, you have your hands full."

"Yes, I do, but it's fun!" I say, smiling. I've heard all this before. In fact, I hear it every time I go anywhere with my brood.

We begin in the produce section, with its wonderful artistically arranged pyramids of fruit. There is something so irresistibly appealing about the apple on the bottom of the pile that a child cannot help but try to touch it. Like a bug to a zapper, the child is drawn to this piece of fruit.

I turn around to the sounds of apples cascading down the display and onto the floor. Like Indiana Jones, there stands my son, holding the all-consuming treasure that he just *had* to get. He's gazing at me with this dumbfounded look, as if to say, "Did you see that??? Wow! I never thought *that* would happen!"

After trying unsuccessfully to dig a hole in the floor so I can hide, I give the offending child an exasperated sigh and say, "Didn't I tell you before we left that I didn't want you taking stuff from the bottom of the pile?"

"You said you didn't want us to take a *can* from the bottom of the pile. You didn't say anything about apples."

With superhuman effort, I resist the urge to send my child hurtling to the moon and instead focus on the positive: my child actually listened to me and remembered what I said! I make a mental note to be a little more specific the next time I give the kids the Lecture.

About this time, a little old man looks at all of us and says, "Are all of those your kids?"

Thinking about the apple incident, I reply, "Nope. They just started following me. I've never seen them before in my life."

On to the bakery section, where everything smells so good I'm tempted to fill my cart with cookies and call it a day. Being on a perpetual diet, I try to hurry past the assortment of pies, cakes, breads, and pastries that have my children drooling. At this point the chorus of "Can We Gets" begins.

Can we get doughnuts? *No.*

Can we get cupcakes? *No.*

Can we get muffins? *No.*

Can we get pie? *No.*

You'd think they'd catch on by this point, but they're just getting started. In the bakery, someone is giving away free samples of coffee cake, and of course my kids all take one. The toddler decides he doesn't like it and spits it out in my hand. That's what moms do: we put our hands in front of our children's mouths so they can spit stuff into them. We'd rather carry around a handful of chewed-up coffee cake than have the child spit it out on the floor. I'm not sure why this is, but ask any mom and she'll tell you the same. Of course, I can't see a garbage can anywhere, so I continue shopping one-handed while searching for someplace to dispose of the regurgitated mess in my hand.

In the meat department, a mother with a baby asks me, "Wow! Are all six yours?" I answer her, "Yes, but I'm thinking of selling a couple of them."

(Still searching for a garbage can at this point.)

After the meat department, my kids' attention spans are spent. They're done shopping by then, but we aren't even halfway through the store. This is when they like to start the shopping-cart races. And who may I thank for teaching them this fun pas-time? My seventh child, also known as my ex-husband. While I'm picking out loaves of bread, the kids are running down the aisle behind the carts in an effort to get us kicked out of the store. I put a stop to that just as my son is about to crash head-on into a giant cardboard cutout of a Keebler elf stacked with packages of cookies.

> *That's what moms do: we put our hands in front of our children's mouths so they can spit stuff into them.*

Eventually I find a small trash can by the coffee machine in the cereal aisle and finally dump out the squishy contents of my hand. After standing in the cereal aisle for an hour and a half while the kids peruse the various cereals, comparing the marsh-mallow and cheap plastic toy contents of all the boxes, I break down and let them each pick out a box. At any given time, we have twenty open boxes of cereal in my house.

Now the baby starts to cry because she's getting hungry. While I debate abandoning the carts and dragging the kids out to the car so I can sit down and feed the baby, she falls asleep in her sling. Hallelujah!

As all this is going on, my toddler is playing Houdini and maneuvering his little body out of the seat belt in an attempt to stand up in the cart. I'm amazed the kid made it to his second birthday without suffering a brain-damaging head injury. Between attempts to flip himself out of the cart, he sucks on the metal bars. Mmmm, can you say influenza?

The shopping trip continues much like this. I break up fights between the kids now and then, and stoop down to pick up items the toddler has flung out of the cart. I desperately try to get everything on my list without adding too many other goodies to the carts.

Somehow I manage to complete my shopping in under four hours and head for the checkouts, where my kids start whining about candy. What evil-minded person had the great idea to put a display of candy in the checkout lanes, right at a child's-eye level? Obviously someone who has never been shopping with children.

As I unload the carts, I notice many extra items that my kids have sneaked into the carts. I remove a box of Twinkies, a package of cupcakes, a bag of candy, and a can of cat food (we don't even have a cat!). As I pay for my purchases, the clerk looks at me, indicates my kids, and asks, "Are they all yours?"

Frustrated, exhausted, sick to my stomach from writing out a check for $289.53, dreading unloading all the groceries and putting them away, and tired of hearing that question, I look at the clerk and answer her in my most sarcastic voice: "No, they're not mine. I just go around the neighborhood gathering up kids to take to the grocery store because it's so much more fun that way."

But I Have Money in My Account . . . Really

You might think that going to the grocery store with only two kids is much easier than going with six. It isn't. You see, when I take all six children to the store with me, the older ones can either help amuse the younger ones or they can help me pick out items from my shopping list. They're also handy to have around because they can unbuckle the little ones from their car seats more easily and quickly than I can. Their little bodies fit more easily into the three-inch space between the driver's seat and the car seat much better than mine does (with my ever-expanding posterior). Although bringing six kids to the grocery store sounds daunting, in some ways it's easier than dragging just two along.

I vividly remember one such shopping trip. My oldest four kids were at school, so I had only my two youngest. What prompted this shopping excursion was the fact that I hadn't been doing much cooking. Martha Stewart I'm not; however, we can live on frozen chicken nuggets and boxed macaroni and cheese for only so long before I start worrying that all the prepackaged and frozen meals are going to stunt my kids' growth. I decided on a couple of menus and made a grocery list so I could do some real cooking.

Okay, in all honesty, this plan came about after my kids and I watched the movie *Ratatouille*, in which a rat living in Paris becomes a wonderfully famous and talented chef. I figured if a cartoon rodent could cook gourmet meals, I should be able to do a little more than boxed mac'n'cheese. Hey, we all have something that motivates us, right?

So I drove to the store. On the way over, Clay, for some unknown reason, was yelling, "Stinky butt! Stinky butt! Stinky butt!" I imagine it was just to annoy me because he knows I can't simultaneously drive and give him threatening "mom looks."

The chorus of "Stinky Butt" continued to a tune eerily like "Funiculi Funicula" as I drove. I was doing a good job remaining calm until my one-year-old, Brooklyn, joined in, sending showers of spit flying as she blew raspberries in time to the "music."

Before I was halfway to the store, I wanted to turn around and go home, but then I'd have to concede that I couldn't cook as well as a Hollywood rat. I was not about to do that. I was on a mission!

I arrived at the grocery store, pulled into an optimal parking space right next to the cart return, and squeezed my more-than-three-inch body into the three-inch space between my seat and the car seats to unbuckle the kids. First I had to put the baby's socks and shoes back on, because really, why wouldn't she have taken them off on the drive? I also wiped the chocolate off my son's face. I didn't even wonder where he'd found chocolate. I know that the kids' car seats house enough old fries, stray M&M's, assorted cracker crumbs, and dust-covered suckers to survive on for a week.

While I was grabbing groceries, the kids were actually pretty good. A little goofy now and then, and a little loud a few times, but great overall. It looked like we would get out of the store without incident, which would have been a personal record.

Then my cell phone rang.

"Hello, Mrs. Meehan. This is—" She didn't even have to complete her sentence, because I recognized that it was the school nurse. I'm pretty sure she has me on speed-dial.

"Hi. Wow, I haven't talked to you in ages! What's it been? Two days?" I sighed. "Which one do you have this time?"

"I have your daughter here. She has a little fever and her ears are hurting."

I looked at my loaded cart and my two relatively peaceful youngest.

"I'll come get her. I'm at the grocery store right now, so it's going to take me a few minutes to get there." The nurse told me not to worry and to take my time.

I debated back and forth in my mind. Should I stop shopping and rush to get my daughter? I was so close to finishing, only a couple of aisles left. If I didn't drop the shopping and leave immediately, how bad of a mom would that make me? And more important, if I skipped the last couple of aisles and rushed to the school, would I ever have a chance to get back out and finish my shopping, or would I be forced to feed my kids meals that a rat wouldn't even eat? I opted to quickly finish up the shopping before heading to the school.

I kicked it into high gear, since the two little ones were losing patience anyway. Clayton kept unbuckling himself from the cart and trying to get out and run all over the store. He was ready to go home. I needed a few more items, though, so I made a game of it in an effort to distract him from his plan to run amok throughout the store.

"I bet I can find the bananas before you can! I'm going to beat you!"

He stopped in his tracks and started looking for bananas.

"You have to sit in the cart and pay attention if you want to find them first."

It worked! He was completely intent on beating me and finding the bananas first. This worked throughout the entire produce section. I discovered long ago that it's always a good idea to have some tricks like this up your sleeves. I've found that Simon Says also works.

"Simon says sit down in the cart. Simon says put your hands on your head. Simon says don't move!"

Another great distraction tool is, "See if you can find something blue. Or something that starts with the letter *B*." If you *really* want to keep them busy for a while, ask them to see if they can find a rhinoceros. You'd be surprised how many times they fall for that.

Eventually, I finished my shopping and raced to the checkouts. Of course, I always seem to pick the slowest line, or the line with the cashier who is in training, or the line with the lady who needs a price check and has twenty bazillion coupons and can't decide how to pay for her purchases. It's inevitable. Unless, of course, I'm by myself and enjoying a nice, leisurely shopping trip. When I'm in no hurry at all, that's when I pick the line with Speedy McSpeederson, cashier extraordinaire.

This time I picked the line where the customer ahead of me was having a price-check problem. I started unloading groceries onto the conveyor belt while trying to get Clay to sit down and stop grabbing at all the candy bars.

"Can I have one, pleeeease?" came his plea.

"You're kidding, right? Halloween was just last week! We have enough candy at home to feed a small nation!"

I grabbed a bag of grapes to set on the conveyor. Because I was distracted, I picked the bag up by the bottom and grapes went flying out of the bag and into my cart. I watched in slow motion as the grapes worked their way through the holes in the cart until they bounced to the floor and scattered everywhere. Why do those plastic bags even have zip tops on them? Never, in all my years on earth, have I seen a zip-top bag of grapes with the top actually closed.

Clayton leapt from the cart and started crawling around on the floor picking up grapes and stuffing them into his mouth. Ugh! By this time, the person in front of the line had paid and moved on. Now I was the annoying lady holding up the line as I scrambled to pick up the grapes before my son could get to them. To get him to stop eating dirty grapes, I bribed him with candy.

"You can have candy when we get home. Just give me the grapes! Stop eating them!" Yes, that's what a good mom says: "Stop eating grapes and I'll give you candy instead."

I finished placing my groceries on the counter and, near tears, begged my children to please just sit still for a couple more minutes. I was feeling guilty for not leaving immediately after the school nurse had called and was worried about my sick daughter's ears. And naturally the cashier was slow. I mean, really slow! I could have driven to Starbucks, bought her a double espresso, and walked back on my hands before she finished with the frozen items alone.

Finally she finished. I swiped my debit card and waited for my receipt. However, the cashier didn't hand me my receipt. Instead, she looked at me like I was pathetic and told me that my card had been declined.

Has this ever happened to you? Do you know that feeling of

embarrassment? My face flushed, my blood pressure went up fifty points, I started sweating, and I lost it with Clay, who was pulling Brooklyn's hair and yelling at the top of his lungs. I felt like my head might explode. In fact, I kind of hoped it would explode so I could take a nice, peaceful ambulance ride out of there.

The thing is, although it's not unusual for my account to be near empty on any given day, I knew I had money in my checking account then. I'd deposited a large check a week before my shopping trip. How could there not be funds? I took my debit card back and quickly scribbled out a check from the same account. I *knew* there was money in the account.

> I felt like my head might explode. . . . I kind of hoped it would explode so I could take a nice, peaceful ambulance ride out of there.

The cashier put my check in the check machine thingy. The machine turned red, smoke came out of it, the lights in the store dimmed, and a spotlight shone down, freezing me in place. A voice boomed over the loudspeaker, "How could you try to pass a bad check in our store, Dawn?!" The people in line behind me all started booing and throwing produce at me.

Okay, maybe that's a slight exaggeration, but the cashier did indeed hand me back my check with the words "This has been declined as well." I meekly asked the cashier if she could suspend my transaction while I called my bank.

I phoned my bank and went through the usual fifteen-minute automated voice menu before I was able to talk to an actual person. I demanded to know what the problem was and why couldn't I use my debit card and they'd better fix it and yadda

yadda yadda. The bank person, after asking for my name, bank account number, social security number, address, hair color, shoe size, and birth city of my mother's first pet, informed me that it could take up to ten business days for out-of-state checks to clear.

"So, let me get this straight. When I deposit a check, it could take two weeks to clear? Yet, when I write a check, it goes through instantaneously? I see. That seems pretty fair."

After my phone call, I rummaged in my purse, hoping to see some cash mysteriously appear. It didn't work. I did, however, find my old debit card. Why did I have two different debit cards, you ask? Well, I hadn't been able to balance my checkbook for over six months, so I gave up and opened a new account. I have the math skills of an eight-year-old, and opening a new account was much easier than trying to figure out why my checkbook had been off by $14.67 for six months. That silly $14.67 was making me nuts. Yes, I know I need help.

Anyway, I hadn't closed my old account and thrown out the old debit card yet, so I handed the old card to the cashier, held my breath, and hoped for the best. It went through! I'm pretty sure there wasn't enough money in that account to cover my purchases, yet somehow it went through. Praise the Lord! My groceries were finally paid for. And now I had to go explain to the school nurse why I was such a bad mom that it took me an hour to get my sick daughter from school.

But on the bright side, at least the animated rats hadn't won. This time, anyway.

Ready, Set, Wait a Minute

Sometimes getting ready to go to the store is even harder than the shopping itself. Before I can go anywhere with my kids, I need to get us all ready to go. That process can take as long as two weeks.

As all parents know, you have to pack a diaper bag before leaving the house. The contents of this diaper bag vary greatly depending on how many children you have and how old they are. For example, a first-time parent of a newborn baby would probably pack a dozen diapers, a box of wipes, a tube of diaper cream, two bibs, two onesies, three sleepers, fifteen toys, two soft books, three burp cloths, extra socks, a hat, booties, a sweater, two blankets, five bottles, a thermometer, a book about baby's first year, the camera, fourteen rolls of film, a camcorder, an infant bathtub, and—finally—the baby, to go to the drive-through at the bank.

It doesn't matter how much stuff I bring along, I always forget something important. I'll walk out the door and forget the whole diaper bag, or my keys, or my purse, or the baby. It's inevitable. One time I left the house and drove straight to my destination without first circling the block and doubling back to the house to retrieve some essential item I'd forgotten. My kids were so confused. They kept asking me where we were going and why we weren't stopping back at home.

Actually, these days, I don't bring so much stuff along when I run errands, but my kids do. For some reason, they're incapable of leaving the house empty-handed. When Brooklyn and I go to pick up the older kids from school, she'll bring her backpack filled with such a hodgepodge of stuff you wouldn't believe. She'll have a Barbie doll, a plastic necklace, five tubes of lipgloss, a sock, a stray puzzle piece, a piece of cheese, nail polish, sunglasses, a hammer, a cookbook, the knob to her dresser drawer that I keep meaning to fix, a half a dozen Legos, an empty juice pouch, and a Band-Aid. You know, because you just never know when you might *need* those things.

Now, I wouldn't mind so much that she dragged those items out to the car, if she'd only carry them back in the house when we arrived home. But noooo. Every item will have been dumped out of the backpack and onto the floor of my van. And they'll sit there. For days, weeks, maybe even months. When I finally get around to cleaning out my van, I need a shovel. You guys are probably laughing because you don't think I'm serious. I've backed into my driveway, opened the back of my van, and put a sign in my yard that reads, "Van Sale." I made $350 last summer, selling everything in my van for 50¢ per item.

So, once the kids have dragged all their belongings into my van and I'm all packed up and ready to go, it's time to strap the kids into their car seats. A word about car seats: although I absolutely *love* the things, they are time consuming. I've had as many as four of my kids in car seats at once. It takes approximately an hour and a half to buckle each one in. You do the math.

As soon as everyone's buckled in and we're ready to go, the call comes from somewhere in the backseat, "I have to go potty!!!!" Despite the twenty times I reminded the kids to use the bathroom before we left the house, someone always has to go right as I'm ready to pull out of the driveway. It's especially fun when it's wintertime and I have to help them take off boots, hats, mittens, snow pants, and coat to go to the bathroom.

When Lexi was younger, she was notorious for the last-minute bathroom breaks. Of course, she always sat in the farthest seat in the back row of the van. To get to her and begin the unbuckling process, I first had to get out, walk around to the sliding door, climb up into the van and across two other kids, and contort my body into a position where I could reach her buckle. (There really should be a physical endurance test for people who are considering having children. Not a single child-rearing book warns you of the flexibility needed for parenting.)

Taking her inside to do her business was not simple because my daughter had a habit of stripping down to nothing in order to pee. Did she just pull down her pants and go? Nope. She had to take off her shirt, socks, shoes, headband, necklace . . . basically everything. There went another forty-five minutes.

Now everyone is ready, and we can get on our way. Nothing can stop us now. But on the way back out to the van, I generally hear screaming and fighting about who's touching who. Something about riding in a car makes kids want to touch, poke, and otherwise bug each other. I think it's because they know I can't do anything about it while I'm driving. They like to watch me try to reach back and flail my arms about wildly while attempting to slap the hand of the one who's doing the poking. But when you have a mom and six kids piled into a car that seats eight, there isn't much room to separate them. I'm thinking of buying a bus.

Eventually we're all buckled up and ready to hit the road. Again. As I turn the key in the ignition, I smell something foul. Either a squirrel crawled into the van and died quite some time ago or the baby has left me a present in her diaper. I get back out of the car to change the baby's diaper, which is a feat in itself.

Anyone who has ever changed a toddler knows this. You lay them down, and the minute you move your hand to reach for a new diaper, the child rolls over and jumps up. Toddlers are quite acrobatic, and despite their short little legs, they have been clocked going eighty miles per hour. I often wish I had even half the energy of a toddler.

I chase her down, carefully drape half my body over her squirmy one, and attempt to remove the soiled diaper without smearing its contents over the floor. The rest of the diaper change resembles wrestling a crocodile. There goes another fifty minutes.

Toddlers are quite acrobatic, and despite their short little legs, they have been clocked going eighty miles per hour.

When I try to strap the toddler back in her car seat, she plays the Stiff as a Board game. You know what I'm talking about? As hard as you try, you cannot get the toddler to bend so you can sit her in her seat. A steel I-beam is more pliable than a toddler who's made up her mind that she doesn't want to be buckled into a car seat. On the opposite end of the spectrum are the toddlers who play the Wet Noodle game. They let their little bodies go limp until it's impossible to get a good hold on them. Toddlers especially like to pull the Wet Noodle in public places while throwing a tantrum.

Okay, now we're *really* ready to go, but alas, I've forgotten where I'm supposed to be going because my children have sucked the brain cells right out of my head. The kids pipe up with, "We're going to the amusement park, remember, Mom?" Ha! I'm not falling for that one. Again.

So, we're off to the grocery store, or school, or the mall, or Grandma and Grandpa's house. Just cruising along in my ultra-cool minivan, jamming to VeggieTales tunes. I've actually forgotten what normal music sounds like.

I have sophisticated friends who say things like "Hey, I just went to see The Black Eyed Peas." I usually answer with something intellectual like, "Really? I love black-eyed peas with ham and collard greens." Whenever people mention the name of some band, I think they're talking about a new vaccine or Hungarian dish or car part. All day long, it's Barney, the Wiggles, and the Backyardigans for me. At least I can brag that I know all the words to "The Yodeling Veterinarian of the Alps," and if your kids ever start singing "The Song That Never Ends," head for the hills.

It's no wonder, after the whole boarding process, that I'm tired before I've even begun my shopping. I think I should start doing my shopping online.

Underwire of Death

It's not just the grocery store that causes so many problems, though; it's pretty much any store of any kind. I vividly remember a particular shopping trip I took a few years ago. I had decided to be brave and go shopping for clothing for myself while dragging along Clay and Lexi (then one and four years old, respectively).

I didn't want to. Believe me. I'd really rather throw myself down the stairs (twice) than take a couple of kids clothes shopping, but when the underwire snapped in my bra, leaving a gaping bloody wound along my armpit, I decided I couldn't afford to put off shopping for a new bra any longer.

Now, I had no intention of actually trying on bras with my little kids in tow. I'm not insane. All I planned to do was grab a couple of bras, buy them, and take them home to try on.

That was the plan. Here's what really happened.

At the store, I had to walk through the kids' section to get to lingerie. As I walked through, I saw the cutest jeans ever for Lexi. I just love shopping for girls. So I spent a good fifteen minutes going through the racks of jeans, looking for her size. I found not one but three cute pairs. I have a bad habit of spending money I hadn't planned on spending.

At this point, Lexi started ducking around the clothes racks, hiding under them. Is there a child on earth who doesn't love to play this game? I remember doing this with my sister when we were kids. In fact I remember a particular time when she and I were shopping with our parents and hiding among the clothes racks. My dad told us to stop acting like wild Indians. My sister and I glanced at each other and without missing a beat, put our hands up to our mouths and started whooping like the proverbial wild Indian. (And I wonder where my kids get their smart-aleck behavior.) Anyway, after walking along hunched over, peeking under the racks for what seemed like an hour, I found her and pulled her out. Meanwhile, Clayton had managed to twist out of the seat belt on the stroller and was standing there ready to flip himself onto his head. I wrestled him back into his stroller while Lexi ducked under a new rack of clothing. I gave Clay a toy from the diaper bag and grabbed my daughter from under the clothing. But because I hadn't learned my lesson, I started looking for shirts to go with the cute jeans.

As I selected some shirts, Clayton launched his toy dolphin at a poor unsuspecting woman and just missed her. Although I'm sure any man would have been proud of his aim and the distance he got on ole Flipper, I was embarrassed and hoped the floor would swallow me. Luckily the shopper just smiled at him.

I'm quite certain that when strangers smile at your kids and tell them how adorable they are, it only fuels their capacity for mischief. I could see the wheels spinning in Clay's head as he thought, *Look at that! I whipped a toy at her and she smiled and said I was just precious! I wonder what would've happened if I'd actually hit her? She probably would've given me candy for that!*

Anyway, I finished picking out clothes for Lexi that will undoubtedly wind up on the floor of her room within a day. Heading toward the register to pay for them, I spotted the absolute cutest little airplane outfit for Clay. Of course I just *had* to get it.

As I plopped the outfit on the back of the stroller, he started screaming at the top of his lungs, *"Pain, pain, pain!"* (which is babytalk for "plane"). People from far and near came to stare at the boy who had been violently injured. I swear I heard an announcement over the PA system asking, "Will the parent of the unruly child in the infants' department please control him?" I quickly slapped my hand over his mouth and pointed out a nice Elmo shirt in an effort to distract him.

I paid for all their clothing and headed toward the lingerie department. Finally. On the way there, Lexi realized that she'd dropped her Barbie doll (the same Barbie doll I told her to leave in the car). She started crying and throwing a fit that brought people running from other parts of the mall to aid the poor child who was apparently being beaten near the lingerie department. When I couldn't settle her down, I half dragged her back to the children's department to search for the missing Barbie.

After crawling around on my hands and knees, much to the delight of Clay, who thoroughly enjoyed ripping every article of clothing he could reach from the racks and throwing them on my back, I found the elusive Barbie. Of course I still couldn't go on to the lingerie department because I had to play stock girl and hang up the dozens of items that Clay had pulled down off the racks.

After only an hour and a half, I finally made it to the lingerie department. At this point, I really didn't care about color or style, because I didn't want to spend another minute in the store. I quickly scanned the racks, searching for something—anything—in my size.

While I was distracted, Clay managed to climb out of the stroller. I saw him escape, but the minute his feet (which have no shoes on them because he apparently tossed them overboard at some point) hit the floor, he was off and running. My daughter squealed with delight and took off after him.

So, there we were, a veritable parade. Clay was laughing and weaving in and out of the racks of bras, occasionally pulling a hanger off the rack and flinging it. Lexi, close behind him, was screaming, "Look, Mom! Boobs! Look at all the boobs!" I was huffing and puffing behind them while I considered turning the other way and just making a dash for the door before anyone realized they belonged to me.

I ended up wearing the bra with the Underwire of Death for another month before I set foot in that store again to buy a replacement. I was afraid that a poster at every cash register displayed my picture and read, "If you see this woman, assume she has her kids with her and is a threat to the peace and tranquility of the mall. Call security immediately."

> Lexi was screaming, "Look, Mom! Boobs! Look at all the boobs!"

But It Looked Cute on the Hanger

Of course, even if I leave the kids at home, shopping isn't as much fun as it used to be. I remember back when a shopping excursion meant a fun outing with my girlfriend. I would spend a ton of money on myself and go out to lunch and have the best time. Those days are long past.

A while back, ABC *World News* asked if they could come out to interview me and film a typical day in the life of a stay-at-home mom of six. Being the calm, cool, collected person I am, I took this phone call in stride and responded with, "What? ABC News? *The* ABC News? You mean, like on TV? You want to film *me*? For real? Is this a joke? Why do you want to talk to me???"

After I hung up, my first thought was *I'm going to need a backhoe and Dumpster to clean up my house before I'll let someone enter with a video camera!* This thought was immediately replaced with *I have nothing to wear!*

Naturally, I called my friend and asked her for some advice. She suggested I wear an interesting piece of jewelry. Hmmm, I thought. Interesting jewelry. I have a painted macaroni necklace the kids made me. That's pretty interesting.

I realized that my wardrobe was seriously lacking in the non–jeans and T-shirts arena, so I figured it was time I did a little clothes shopping.

Now, I don't particularly care for clothes shopping. I look forward to shopping for clothing as much as I look forward to my kids coming home from school in the afternoon—it's fun for the first few minutes. I actually enjoy perusing the racks of clothing. I don't mind searching for my size from among the possibilities.

Taking the clothes into the dreaded dressing room and trying them on is the part I could live without.

This time, I left my kids at home so I could take my time and do a little clothes shopping by myself. The store I went to had this really great feature in the dressing rooms. Perhaps you've witnessed this feature yourself. It's a doorbell. A *very. Loud. Doorbell.*

When I walked into the room, *Ding dong* sounded loudly enough for people in the next state to hear. Why do they do this? Why do they need a doorbell? I've never once, in my entire life, seen a dressing room attendant run to the entrance and say, "Oh hello! I heard the doorbell and thought I'd come welcome you to the dressing rooms!" In fact, come to think of it, I don't believe I've ever seen a dressing room attendant period, let alone one who would run to greet you.

So, after sustaining permanent damage to my hearing, I took the clothing that I thought looked very nice on the hangers into an open room. I pushed aside the mountain of clothes left behind by a person who apparently couldn't bother to remove the clothes from the room and hang them on the return rack. I mean, trying on clothing can be exhausting. Clearly the patron before me didn't have the strength to gather up her items and walk the four whole feet out of the room to the return rack. Perfectly understandable.

Although, to be honest, other people's laziness has come in handy for me several times. On more than one occasion, I've been in a dressing room and seen a top left in the room by the previous occupant, tried it on, and ended up liking it better than the stuff I actually brought in with me.

Anyway, amid the piles of clothing, in front of the wonderful three-paneled mirrors, in the dressing room's glorious fluorescent lighting, I began the depressing ritual of trying to convince myself that I didn't look quite as bad as the mirrors were telling me. Am I the only one who always takes three identical pairs of pants in three different sizes to the dressing room? I don't think there's an industry standard for women's pants. I could wear three different sizes in three different brands, and I never know which will fit, so I generally bring in three pairs to try on. It's much better than walking in and out of the room looking for a different size and hearing the stupid doorbell again and again.

I tried on the largest pair first and then exclaimed, loudly enough for everyone else to hear, "Oh these pants are *huge* on me! I need a smaller size." After getting that out of the way, it didn't seem so bad when I tried on a pair so small that I required medical attention after attempting to button them.

While I was trying on clothes that were clearly marked with the wrong size—I couldn't possibly have grown a whole size since the last time I went shopping, a year ago—the annoying doorbell went off again and again and again. The one time I get out without out my kids, and someone else's kids were running back and forth through the doorway, making the doorbell sound repeatedly. I resisted my urge to shout, "Knock it off!" and instead concentrated on how thankful I was not to be trying on swimsuits today. Now *that* makes for a depressing day.

After pulling on pair after pair of pants and shirt after

> I was trying on clothes that were clearly marked with the wrong size — I couldn't possibly have grown a whole size since the last time I went shopping.

shirt, turning this way and that, examining myself in the mirror, sucking in my stomach until I felt light-headed, standing on my tiptoes to fool the mirror into thinking I was taller, and realizing that my gray roots really needed to be touched up again, I called it a day. I came home with a few items . . . which were on sale, by the way.

I generally judge my shopping spree not by what I bought but by how much I saved on what I bought. I have a friend who is the Queen of the Bargain. Seriously, she should teach classes. I don't know anyone else who can come home from shopping with two pairs of jeans, a sweater, three tops, four new throw pillows, a necklace and bracelet set, a handbag, and two pairs of shoes for $1.99 plus tax. I envy her skill.

After arriving home from my big shopping excursion, I hung my finds from the knob on my dresser. I kept looking at them, disliking them more every time I passed by. In the end, I ended up returning half of it, even though I knew I'd have to start over and the chances that I could find time to go by myself again were slim. If you thought grocery shopping with the kids was bad, try tugging on some jeans with one hand while holding on to your toddler with the other so he can't crawl under the dressing room door, all the while keeping the door shut with your foot because the lock is broken and the baby keeps trying to open the door from her seat in the stroller. Or chasing your toddler in and out of the racks of clothing while you distractedly try to find your size. It makes taking the kids to the grocery store look like a walk in the park.

Don't even get me started about the times I've taken all six kids to the park. . . .

· · · · · · · · · · ·

Chapter Three

I Was the Perfect Parent Until I Had Kids

When you're expecting your first baby, you worry about doing everything just right. You envision an idyllic world where you raise the perfect child, who never talks back, wouldn't dream of running around like a banshee in public, gets straight As, wins the Nobel Peace Prize, marries the most wonderful person in the world, and provides you with perfect grandchildren. At this stage, when you see children misbehaving in public, you're certain your kids will *never* act like that.

Come on, we've all done it. Before having kids, you told yourself that *you* would never do such and such with *your* kids. *Your* kids would never misbehave. *Your* kids would always listen and never talk back and they'd keep their rooms clean and they'd never shout or burp or run in the house. *You'd* never give *your* child candy or sit them in front of the television to get an hour of peace and quiet. *You'd* never threaten to ground *your* kids until the second coming.

And then you have kids.

I remember watching, appalled, as someone fed their one-year-old fast food from McDonald's. At some point, however, I changed my mind, as I'm pretty sure French fries were my sixth child's first solid food.

Before I had children, I remember seeing kids throw themselves down in all-out temper tantrums in the middle of a store. I swore that *my* kids would *never* behave so poorly in public. Of course, it wasn't long after that I had to physically remove my son from a toy store at my local mall, pulling him by his arms, his body limply dragging across the floor as onlookers judged me as completely incompetent.

I'm pretty sure French fries were my sixth child's first solid food.

I have a friend whose first three children were very laid back, easygoing, mellow babies. They slept through the night right away. As toddlers, they didn't have temper tantrums. As young children, they didn't get into stuff and make messes all day. She had the whole parenting thing down to a science and couldn't understand why others claimed to have a hard time dealing with their children's behavior. Then she had her fourth baby, who is part monkey. She suddenly knew what other parents were talking about when they complained about their children climbing the furniture to get into stuff.

I've learned my lesson in judging other parents. Every child and every family is different. We all want to do what's best for our children and our families, but when you're in the midst of the messiness of family life, your expectations change. Your kids aren't perfect. You're not going to do everything right. And it's okay. Even after six kids, I'm still learning.

Childproofing and Other Lies

When you're expecting your first child, you'll do anything to guarantee you'll be a good parent. You take classes on diapering, breastfeeding, and caring for your baby. You take classes that promise you won't feel the excruciating pain of childbirth if only you breathe. You take classes on childproofing your home.

That is the one that did me in. After I took the childproofing class, I remember taking out a loan, going to the local baby store, and buying every item in the store that promised to make my home safe for babies and toddlers. Of course, now that I have six children, I look back and wonder why they don't sell products to keep your house safe *from* babies and toddlers!

But back when I was expecting my first, I had hopes of being the perfect mother and raising my baby in the perfect, safe environment. In other words, I had no clue. So I loaded up my shopping cart with a dozen of every babyproofing item I could find.

When my baby was a year old, harsh reality smacked me upside the head and I realized the whole "babyproofing" industry was a scam. They don't want you to know the truth, but I'm going to spill the beans. Here it is in a nutshell: *there is no such thing as childproof.*

There. It's been said. The fact is, where there's a will, there's a way. If a child wants it badly enough, the child *will* find a way to get to it, whether your house is childproofed or not.

Those childproof nightlights? The child just grabs a screwdriver (like they saw you do when you installed the thing) and tries to open it that way. The screwdrivers are way up high where the child won't reach them, you say? Think again. All he has to do is push a kitchen chair over, climb up on it, and voilà, he has a screwdriver. Hmmmm . . . a child, a screwdriver, and an outlet. Now *there's* a combination!

How about those nifty little cabinet locks? The child learns (before she learns to walk or talk) how to open the cabinet just enough to squeeze her little fingers in there and depress the latch, thus releasing the cabinet door. The magnetic cabinet locks? I admit these are better than most locks. That is, until the child finds where you keep the magnet and opens the cabinet with it. Then she'll undoubtedly lose the magnet, leaving you to take the door off its hinges to access the inside. If you're really lucky, before she loses the magnet, she'll use it to irreversibly turn the television screen all sorts of fun rainbow colors.

The bumper pad around the coffee table? *If* the pad manages to stay on once the child figures out it's removable, it really doesn't provide the protection necessary for a child who runs into the table at a full sprint.

I like some products, though. Car seats are great. They help ensure that your little ones will be safe and secure in the case of a car accident. They didn't have car seats when I was a child. I cannot begin to imagine driving along with my children bouncing around in the back of my car. How did my parents do it?

But the greatest thing about car seats is that they keep your children pinned in one spot! They just don't go far enough. I think manufacturers ought to market a version of the car seat to use inside your house. You know, something like a little La-Z-Boy with a five-point harness. How great would that be? Never again would you sneak a shower only to step out of the bathroom four minutes later to a kitchen covered in whipped cream, the dog foaming at the mouth trying to clean up the whipped cream, and the kids skating in their socks through the whole mess (not that this has ever happened to me, of course). You could take a leisurely shower and even shave your legs and apply moisturizer. When you stepped out of the bathroom, your children would be where you left them, strapped into their seats, coloring on actual coloring books (because they couldn't reach the walls from where their seats were positioned). I think I'm on to something here. I'm pretty sure there's a big market for this product of the future. Someone, get on that, will ya?

I used to keep a bowl filled with candy on the top of my refrigerator so the kids wouldn't be able to get into it. And I kept my knife block full of sharp knives up there for the same reason. I thought they were out of harm's way, until I learned that my three-year-old could actually scale my refrigerator to steal the candy. As soon as I realized this, I knew I needed to move the items. But to where? Where on earth could I put dangerous knives or tempting candy so that my kids wouldn't be able to get at them? The kitchen cabinets? Nope. The garage? Nope. The laundry room? Nope. Peru? Maybe that would be safe.

Sometimes childproofing means keeping things that aren't necessarily dangerous out of harm's way. One night a few years ago, I was trying to help Austin with his homework. When you have more than one child, you have to develop strategies to keep them all occupied at the same time. I've found that duct-taping them to the wall works nicely. So on this particular night I thought I had everything under control. Savannah was reading a book, Jackson was in a trance playing a video game, and I was sitting at the table with Austin, feeling stupid that I couldn't help him with his fourth-grade math. (I'm convinced that fourth-grade math is the reason my kids think they're smarter than me in every aspect of life. They figure that if I can't help them with their math homework, I must be stupid and incapable of knowing pretty much anything.)

Anyway, everything was going smoothly. Everyone was occupied with an activity, no one was fighting, nothing was being broken, and the planets were all aligned in harmony. Even Lexi, then three years old, and Clayton, then one year old, were playing quietly with blocks in Clay's room.

Then it hit me. Playing quietly is almost never a good thing. Where there's quiet, there's mischief.

I cannot stress this enough. You really shouldn't ever sit back, relax, and revel in the silence.

> When you have more than one child, you have to develop strategies to keep them all occupied at the same time. I've found that duct-taping them to the wall works nicely.

You will regret this when you discover that the silence you were just enjoying was a product of the kids focusing their attention on their latest science experiment.

While you were daring to sip that glass of iced tea and thumb through a magazine that you've been meaning to get to for a year and a half, the kids were precariously stacking furniture, cartoon style, to see how high they could climb before toppling to the floor. Or perhaps you take a moment of silence to make a couple of phone calls. When you get off the phone, you'll no doubt find the kids testing the suction power of the vacuum on the dog. In any case, it's not a good idea to enjoy the silence.

So after it hit me that my two little ones were being exceptionally quiet, I peeked in to check on them. As I opened the door, the stench of diaper cream hit me. My two small children were literally covered in thick white goo. *Great*, I thought, *my kids are mimes.* Even their hair was white! Two pairs of eyes peeked out from masks of pure white. Four little hands, covered in gloves of white cream, were busily smearing yet more cream on the walls in a sort of larger-than-life mural of a polar bear in a snowstorm. Wonderful! I had a new mess to clean up!

At least I got out of doing math for a while. My little ones were grinning from ear to ear, so proud of the lovely new hairdos and moisturizing treatments they had given each other. Now, how can you be mad at little smiling white clown faces?

I learned, after washing their hair four times with dishwashing liquid, that you never, ever, never, ever leave diaper cream within a toddler's reach. It must be kept locked up in Peru with the cleaning supplies, rat poison, and weed killer.

I keep telling myself that my kids aren't mischief makers; they're brilliant explorers. They aren't naughty for scaling Mount Refrigerator; they're getting exercise and learning rock-climbing skills. I try to convince myself that they aren't just rotten and sneaky; they're amazingly smart to be able to figure out how to get what they want. They must be geniuses if they can operate childproof locks when I can't figure them out myself. These are good skills to have, right? My kids will probably all turn out to be rocket scientists, right? Right? Come on, someone agree with me!

It's truly amazing to watch the wheels turn in a child's head.

Watching a child learn through exploring, tasting, touching, smelling, and listening is an awesome thing. Children love testing the laws of physics. They're enthralled with hands-on experiments to see how the world works. Their brains are like little sponges just soaking up everything; and no matter how well you try to childproof, they can usually find a way around it to check things out and get into mischief.

The trick, I've discovered, is finding a way to look beyond the mess they made and all the money you wasted on childproofing and try to understand the reason for the mess. So the kitchen floor is covered with water and the freezer door is hanging open. When you finish flipping out about the mess, you might be surprised to learn that the kids poured water on the floor and opened the freezer door so the cold air would freeze the water to give them an indoor ice rink. That's pretty ingenious, actually. If my children don't grow up to be the rocket scientists I think they'll be, I might have to rethink my theory, but for now, I'm just going to enjoy it.

Budding Artists
(Graffiti Counts as Art, Doesn't It?)

Before I had kids, I never expected my house to turn into an art gallery. It's kind of an abstract aesthetic these days, but I like to think it's my way of showcasing the budding creativity in our midst.

For some reason, markers have a way of multiplying in my house. I'm not sure how this happens, but much like the heads on the Hydra fought by Hercules, for every Sharpie I toss into the garbage, two more appear. I've confiscated numerous markers over the years, but the kids have ways of finding more. I think I've spent at least two years of my life trying to scrub marker off the walls.

Only one of two things can happen when you attempt to clean marker from a wall. The first thing that happens is often nothing. After an hour of scrubbing, nothing happens; the marks stay right where they were so artistically applied: on the wall. Or sometimes the marks do come off the wall. Of course the paint washes off the wall right along with the marks, but you have to take the good with the bad, right? Needless to say, every wall in my house either has marker artwork or bleached-out patches with no paint. Some walls have both! It just adds to the Early American Disaster décor in my house.

Having the walls colored on by your kids really isn't so bad when you compare it to the other surfaces they can decorate. For example, there's carpet. If you think getting marker off a wall is difficult, try scrubbing it out of carpeting sometime. When I bought the carpeting that's in my family room, I walked into the store and told the salesman, "I want carpeting that looks like it's been thrown up on, walked on with muddy shoes, and had corn-flakes ground into it, so when those things really *do* happen, it'll blend." Judging by the salesman's expression, they don't get that request too often.

> Having ~~Coloring~~ the walls colored on by your kids really isn't so bad when you compare it to the other surfaces they can decorate.

Although I have camouflage carpeting in my family room, marker shows up quite well on the carpeted areas throughout the rest of the house. I have found that strategically placing a houseplant, end table, or floor lamp over the marker covers it nicely. Sometimes it's preferable to let the kids dump piles of clothing over their floors instead of making them put away their clothes; clothing on the floor covers all sorts of mysterious stains on the carpeting.

Another place my kids like to draw is on themselves. My kids just love decorating themselves and each other with marker tattoos. Because I don't get enough attention when I take all six kids to the store, the kids like to make themselves stand out even more by drawing mustaches and beards on their faces, dinosaurs on their arms, and random scribbles up and down their legs.

Sitting in the doctor's waiting room one time, bored to tears, my oldest kids decided to entertain themselves by decorating Clayton with a black marker beard, mustache, and big, round eyeglasses. And then there's the time Austin drew a picture of a *T. rex* on Jackson's back. His entire back. The folks at Miami Ink would've been impressed. With any luck, my kids will get this out of their systems now, and won't go out when they're teenagers and get crazy tattoos they'll later regret.

I especially love it when the kids sign their name to their artwork.

"Why did you draw this picture on the *wall?*"

"I didn't do it."

"Really? That's interesting. I wonder why it has your name next to the picture."

"I don't know. Someone else must have done that."

"Uh-huh. That sounds likely."

Of course you can tell who did the artwork by judging the sophistication of the drawing. If the offending marks are just random scribbles, you can bet the baby did it. If the walls are covered with people who look like potatoes with arms, legs, and eyes, you're pretty safe to assume the toddler did it. If the artwork looks more like the Sistine Chapel, you can safely guess that the teenager . . . , actually, scratch that. If it looks like the Sistine Chapel, just leave it and hope it distracts visitors from the potato people drawn on the carpet.

Finding marker drawings in new and interesting places such as the back of the leather chair in the family room and the side of the refrigerator can be nerve-racking. But that's only the beginning.

You're Wearing *That?*

In the days B.C. (before children), I'd see kids in the store wearing the craziest outfits and I'd say to myself, *What on earth were their parents thinking???* Now that I have kids of my own, I understand. Kids like to dress themselves, and it usually just isn't worth fighting over.

So your child wants to wear a red velour sweatshirt, purple plaid pants (I'm not sure why anyone would have purple plaid pants to begin with . . .), yellow knee socks, snow boots, and a tiara in July. So what? As a parent, you have to pick and choose your battles. Generally it's best to save your energy for more important things, such as when the kids want to build a spaceship from parts they've taken out of your car, or when they decide to paint their bedroom door with nail polish. Fighting over clothes just isn't worth it.

Clothing six kids who outgrow things daily can be exceedingly expensive. I've tried shopping at resale shops, I've bought clothes on clearance for a fraction of their original price at the end of the season, and I've always happily accepted hand-me-downs. But I think I might just stop buying new clothes for my kids entirely. It's not like they appreciate them.

Austin wears the same nasty old T-shirts day in and day out. It doesn't matter that he has a closet full of nice, new clothes. I'm sure his teacher thinks he's an orphan. And when I take away the shirts and toss them in the garbage, they somehow magically reappear in his drawer again and again. I've given up on jeans lasting more than a week with him. Apparently there's some sort of mysterious force field at school that causes perfectly good jeans to get holes in the knees, because that boy can't manage to keep a new pair of jeans intact for more than a day.

Savannah has nothing to wear. Again, she has a closet full of beautiful, untouched clothing, but I guess the clothes are invisible to her, because when she opens her closet door, she sees nothing. She used to wear my shoes all the time, but she's since outgrown them, thankfully. Hmmm . . . maybe I could go raid *her* closet for things to wear.

Jackson used to spend most of his day just hanging out in his pajamas or occasionally his underwear. I'm sure walking around in nothing but your PJs is comfortable. Can you imagine the look on the poor mailman's face if I answered the door in my undies? I'm sure I'd make quite an impression at PTO meetings! Nowadays, Jackson has to make sure his boxers are sticking out of his pants. Why is this? Why do boys want their underwear showing on purpose? I really

> Savannah has nothing to wear. She has a closet full of beautiful, untouched clothing, but when she opens her closet door, she sees nothing.

don't understand this. I'm forever telling him to pull up his pants. "Do you need a belt? I can get you a belt. *Please* wear a belt!"

Lexington likes the name-brand clothing, which is fine with me as long as it is secondhand. She can wear anything she wants and it'll look good on her. No, I'm not envious of her model-thin frame. Well, maybe a little bit. She's definitely the fashion plate of the family. Even as a toddler, she was the one to wear leotards, bathing suits, Little Mermaid costumes, and enough jewelry to make Mr. T jealous wherever she went.

Clayton wears whatever I pick out for him. The only problem is, he likes to dress himself, and 99 percent of the time he puts things on the wrong way. I mean, he has a fifty-fifty shot of getting it right, yet his shoes are always on backward and the tag is always sticking out the front of his shirt. I have no idea why this is.

And little Brooklyn doesn't care what she's wearing as long as she has shoes on. Even as a baby, she would wake up and bring me her shoes. Before I changed her diaper, I had to slip shoes onto her feet. Her favorites are these bright pink cowboy boots. She wears those everywhere every day. In her world, pink cowboy boots go with absolutely everything. When she turned four, I had pictures taken of her wearing her pink cowboy boots with a T-shirt and a tutu. I wanted to look back and remember the goofy way she dressed at that age.

All babies tend to go through clothing like it's going out of style, but I think Clayton went through more clothing changes than any other kid ever. I remember one day in particular. It was Lexi's birthday party, and he destroyed her cake by landing on it. Before I could reach him, he lunged for her cake, leaving a huge hole in it. As I quickly grabbed his right hand, which was already full of cake, he grabbed a fistful of cake with his left hand. Have you ever tried holding a squirming toddler while attempting to immobilize both of his sticky, icing-covered hands? I don't recommend it.

That was Clayton's second change of clothing for the day (the first being the change from his pajamas). Technically, I didn't change him that time. When I went to get him out of his crib in the morning, there he was, stark naked, jammies flung overboard and diaper stuck between the bars on the crib. Thankfully, it was only a wet diaper that time.

The next change of clothing came when Lexi took him outside, led him to the sandbox, and proceeded to pour wet sand on his head, down his shirt, and in his diaper. Change number three.

After that, I let him run around in his room while I put away some clean clothes. As soon as he was free of me, he made a beeline for the dog's dish and dumped the contents down his shirt. Change number four.

At lunch he used half a peanut butter sandwich as a styling aid in his hair and smeared the other half on his shirt. After a bath and several hair scrubbings, I changed him yet again.

At naptime, I sat down, cuddled my nice, clean baby, and started to give him a bottle. I apparently didn't have the cap screwed on tightly enough, and milk started to leak out, drenching his shirt. Here we go again. . . .

The rest of the day was fairly uneventful. Clayton played, had fun, and got dirty. Before bed, I gave him a bath and changed him into his jammies. Then I let him go while I hung up his towel. He ran straight for the tub, which I hadn't yet drained, and flung himself in. Ack! Did you know that your standard disposable diaper holds fifty gallons of liquid? Let's just say that after he jumped in, I no longer had to drain the tub.

So, eight clothing changes later, he went to bed. And I wonder how I accumulate so much dirty laundry!

The Most Glorious Time of the Year

Before I had kids, I was quite certain that they would never get in trouble at school. Only children of awful parents got in trouble with their teachers, and I was *not* going to be an awful parent. Imagine my surprise when things didn't go according to my plan.

I'm not one to dance. Really. I never have been one to "cut a rug." Trip over the rug? Yes. Trip the light fandango? Notsomuch.

One time of the year, however, I shed my inhibitions and proudly strut my coordination-impaired abilities for all who care to watch. That time, my friends, is back-to-school time.

Yes, that glorious time of year when the pencils are sharpened, the notebooks are fresh and new, just waiting for inspiration, and the lunch bags don't smell like feet. Ahhhh—glorious Back to School Time!

After I ~~kick~~ lovingly send the kids on their way, I've been known to dance a jig that would have Michael Flatley weeping with unbridled jealousy.

Preparing for back-to-school time is always fun, even though we have to pay a hefty registration fee for each child attending "public" school and fill lengthy supply lists for each child. It takes about a month to collect all the items each kid is required to bring to the first day of school, especially the few brand-specific, hard-to-find things that are always on their lists. Now I'm up to six backpacks, five lunch boxes, one hundred pencils, and a small forest's worth of paper, not to mention the glue, red pens, highlighters, clipboards, folders, book covers, tissues, zip-top bags, hand sanitizer, and enough paper towels to soak up Lake Michigan.

But one specific first day of school a few years ago made me wonder why I even bother. I picked up my darlings after the bell rang and attempted the futile process of asking the kids how their days were.

"What did you do today?" I asked optimistically.

"Nothing," came the general answer from the bunch.

"What did you have for lunch?" I packed their lunches and knew very well what was in them, but I was on a mission to find out something, anything, about their day.

"I don't remember," came another vague reply.

"Are any of your friends in your class this year?"

"I don't know," came the succinct reply.

Still forging ahead, determined to get a little information, I asked, "Do your teachers seem nice?"

"I guess so. She hasn't started yelling yet," Austin answered.

"Do you have homework?"

"I don't know," they answered.

Apparently their brains were sucked out at school.

Really, why do I bother to ask them this stuff? I think it must be written in the mother's handbook somewhere that we have to ask these things even though we know we'll never get an actual answer.

I think it must be written in the mother's handbook somewhere that we have to ask these things even though we know we'll never get an actual answer.

Unless, of course, you have one of those kids who actually

likes to talk about their day. I have one of those. On this first day of school, Savannah told me about her day in great detail. Although the others didn't remember a single thing that happened at school, Savannah proceeded to tell me everything. "It was so great. We went out for recess. Do you know Katie? Katie was wearing this purple shirt with a monkey on it today. It was so funny. She went down the slide and hurt her hand. I had to walk with her to the nurse's office. She's nice. She put ice on it. I didn't get to stay with Katie. I had to go back to class. You know who's in my class? Rob. He got in trouble for calling someone a name. I like Harry Potter. We have Harry Potter brooms hanging from the ceiling in our classroom. You can't really fly on them, though. They're for decoration. Alex says he read all the Harry Potter books, but he's lying because he can't even read *The Cat in the Hat*. Whatcha doing? Can I help? My teacher says I'm a good helper. I got to bring the attendance to the office today. You know who was in the office? . . ."

In the midst of all that, as I was attempting to cook dinner, Austin said to me, "I got in trouble today."

Now Austin likes to joke around, so I didn't believe him at first. I was thinking that he couldn't possibly have gotten into trouble. It's only the *first* day of school after all. How could he possibly be in trouble on the first day?

"Very funny," I told him.

"No, I really did get in trouble. I had to stay in for recess," he insisted.

"Please tell me you're kidding and you didn't really get in trouble on the first day of school," I whined.

"Okay, I'm kidding," he tried to appease me. "But I really did get in trouble," he reiterated.

Exasperated, I said sarcastically, "That's just wonderful. What did you do?"

"I called my friend Jimmy a name."

"What did you call him?"

"A sissy horse."

"A sissy horse?" A sissy horse? "Where do you come up with this stuff?"

I couldn't believe it. A sissy horse? What does that even mean? I pray that someday he will learn to use his creativity for good, not evil. Until then, I guess I'll just resign myself to being continually amazed at the, uh, *creative* stuff the kids say. And of course making sure no one else is around to hear it.

It Grows Back

I've never been able to find a foolproof place to hide scissors from my children. They always manage to find them somehow, and they always have to immediately try them out. I've found papers cut to shreds, bed sheets with cuts in them, and locks of hair on the floor. I think all my kids have either given a haircut to a sibling, friend, a doll, or themselves or they have received a haircut from a sibling or friend.

Austin played barber to Savannah and gave her a little trim when she was two years old. A year later, Savannah gave herself a haircut after watching the Disney movie *Mulan*. The girl in the movie cuts off her hair so she'll look like a boy. Apparently that sounded like a great idea to Savannah, who took the scissors and cut off a big chunk of hair from right at the front of her head. She had quarter-inch bangs for quite a while. Stylish.

Lexington, not wanting to be left out of The World's Worst

Haircuts Archives, gave herself a trim not once, but twice! Right before she was to be the flower girl in my sister's wedding, I discovered locks of blonde hair on the floor. I went to search for the culprit and found my daughter with hair down to her waist on one side and up to her ear on the other. I had nightmarish flashbacks of the haircut I gave my Cathy Quick Curl doll when I was a little kid.

I looked at her hair and calmly asked her, "WHAT ON EARTH DID YOU DO?!?!?!" She started crying and repeated "I hate my short hair," again and again. I instantly felt bad for yelling and tried to calm her down. I mean, it's just hair after all. But the poor thing looked ridiculous. I took her to the beauty shop to get it trimmed and evened out. The hairdresser felt so bad for my daughter, who was still crying over her haircut, that she put butterfly clips and glitter spray in her hair. At first I thought that was very nice of her.

I soon changed my mind, however. The next day, Lexi found another pair of scissors and went to town on her hair yet again. When I asked her why she had cut her hair again, she said, matter of factly, "So I can go get more glitter hairspray, Mommy." Well, of course that's why. Grrr.

But Austin has had the most unusual haircuts. One year, we were standing in line at the zoo to get some ice cream and we saw a teenager with a mohawk. I said to him, *jokingly*, "Hee hee hee, how would you like to have hair like that?" Now he was *supposed* to answer me, "Moooom! No way!!!" But

> When I asked her why she had cut her hair again, she said, matter of factly, "So I can go get more glitter hairspray."

nooooo, my little smart-aleck comment backfired on me when he answered, "Cool! Yeah!!!"

So I did what any other normal mother would do: I told him he was out of his mind and he couldn't possibly wear his hair like that or people would think he was a freak, and more important, they would think *I* was a freak for letting my seven-year-old son wear his hair like some punk rocker.

The next day, my son showed up at his baseball game sporting, yes, you guessed it, a mohawk. After listening to him complain for hours that he really, really, really, really wanted a mohawk, I decided that this was a battle not worth fighting. It's hair. Hair grows back. No big deal, right? So he wants to go around with hair that looks like a Roman helmet. What's it going to hurt?

Before I had kids, I would have looked at that boy with the mohawk and thought, "That poor boy. His parents don't care about him." Now I understand the truth: that his parents love him enough to let him look like a fool.

It's good to let your kids express themselves. It's okay if they want to try out different looks, especially with hair and clothing. Those things aren't permanent and can be a fun way for kids to discover who they are. I reverted back to my saying, "Pick and choose your battles." I figure I can use this in the future when he asks me for something outrageous.

"Can I have a pet hippopotamus?"

"No, son."

"You never let me have anything I want!"

"That's not true. Remember that time I let you have a mohawk?"

End of discussion.

It's a Hot Dog!

Of course, I'd rather find a little lock of hair here and there than old food items stashed around the house. There's nothing quite so disgusting as coming across an old sandwich so moldy you could open a penicillin factory with it. I once found such a sandwich in my sons' room. It had taken on a life of its own. Its name was Bob. It was about to take over our town.

A few years ago, I was cleaning my sons' room while conversing with a gentleman on the phone. I can never just talk on the phone. No, I have to sweep the floor, clean the toilet, wash dishes, or fold laundry while chatting. So I was on the phone talking to a gentleman, a businessman in the corporate world who was kind enough to call me between a luncheon with a client and a business meeting to give me some advice.

As I was talking to him (and, of course, picking up toys in the boys' room), I saw, to my horror, some sort of food-type object. At first I wasn't sure what it was. I thought maybe it was a Tootsie Roll, but it wasn't quite the right color. It occurred to me that perhaps it wasn't really food! Oh no, please don't let it be . . . Whew! It wasn't anything that belonged in a toilet, thankfully.

Upon closer inspection, I realized it was a chunk of a hot dog. A petrified hot dog. You could easily see that it had been in the boys' room since sometime around the Mesozoic Era. In the middle of my phone call with this important gentleman, I shrieked, "It's a hot dog! I just found a petrified hot dog in my boys' room!" I'm pretty sure the man thinks I have brain damage.

This is not the only time I've found food in strange places around the house. I've found dried-up string cheese in the laundry basket, fruit snacks wedged in the couch cushions, dried apple slices and brown squishy bananas on the floor of my car (actually, I probably have enough food on the floor of my car to make an entire Happy Meal), half-eaten waffles on the bookshelf, and sippy cups full of what was once milk but has since turned to cottage cheese under the couches. Here's a tip: Do not open a sippy cup that has been lost for more than one day, especially if you have a weak stomach. You should promptly throw away the entire cup in a trash receptacle far from your house. The next state should be far enough away.

One time, while tucking Clayton in bed, I found half a hot dog bun under his bunk.

"Why do you have a nasty old bun under your bed?" I asked him.

"I don't know" was his well-thought-out answer.

"Remember when I talked to you about bringing any kind of food into your room? You can't take food in your room. It belongs in the kitchen only."

He replied, "I know, you said if I put food in my room, ants and bugs and mice will come in my room."

"That's right! You *do* remember. So why did you put this bun in your room?"

"Because you said that ants and mice will come in my room!"

It hit me then that my little speech about visiting critters didn't deter him from bringing food into his room. Quite the contrary, he was now sneaking food under his bed in an effort to *attract* critters! It simply amazes me how their minds work sometimes.

"Why did you put this bun in your room?"

I remember when I was a kid, I'd sometimes take huge mouthfuls of peas or some other dreaded vegetable and then I'd ask to be excused from the table so I could run to the bathroom to spit the offending veggies into the toilet. My kids aren't quite so clever, however.

> "Because you said that ants and mice will come in my room!"

They take their napkins full of chewed-up, spit-out food, and they stash them around the house, in various places such as the bookcase, their closets, and behind the toilet. I once found a slice of pizza hidden in a toy safe in my son's room. Unfortunately I discovered it many months after the pizza was locked safely away. It was so rotted, I didn't even recognize it as pizza until I had forensic testing done on it. And why did my son put the pizza in his safe to begin with? Was he planning for a rainy day? Perhaps he thought he'd save it for some night when I prepared something for dinner that he didn't like. Or maybe he was just stashing it away in case he got the midnight munchies. Maybe this hoarding of food is a result of living with five siblings. In any case, it wasn't a pretty sight.

My vehicle is a great place for interesting food finds. I especially love it when I get in my minivan after it has sat unused for a week in 90-degree weather and I'm greeted with the stench of rotting bananas or moldy apples. I think the absolute worst smell I've ever had the misfortune of experiencing was when Jackson left a package of onion rings from Sonic in my car. We'd all been noticing the smell that was getting funkier and funkier as time passed, but I couldn't pinpoint the source. Finally, after almost vomiting from the stench while unloading groceries from the back of my van one hot July day, I searched the vehicle high and low. That's when I discovered the decomposing onion rings hidden under one of the seats. I used a pressure washer and a gallon of bleach to disinfect my van after that. By the way, you couldn't pay me to eat onion rings after that incident.

No car seat would be complete without the requisite cracker and cereal crumbs. And I'd be confused if my car didn't contain at least four squished fruit snacks on the seats or a dozen fries scattered about the floor. I think all the food strewn about my car may have attracted some squirrels who now live in the backseat. The good news is that if we're ever stranded in a snowstorm, we could live off the crumbs and scraps for a good month.

I've found all sorts of stuff in the floor registers of my kids' rooms, as well. At one point there were about five million Cheerios, Matchbox cars, a dried-out piece of string cheese, and a dozen pennies. A couple years ago, I hired a company to clean out the ductwork. As the worker vacuumed out each register, I heard clunking and rattling sounds. He was obviously sucking up more than just dust. When he had finished, he told me, "I think I might have sucked up some of your kids' toys."

"No kidding, huh?"

He walked outside to empty out the vacuum and returned, saying, "You know what I found in the vacuum?"

"Jimmy Hoffa?"

"No. A pair of underwear." He handed me a small pair of underwear with Cinderella on it.

"Well, of course you did. I wouldn't expect anything less from my kids." The toys, food, underwear, and wrappers aren't exclusive to the registers. Oh no. One time I found nearly thirty Tootsie Roll wrappers in my son's bed.

"Why were you eating candy in bed?"

"I wasn't."

"Really? Then why are all these wrappers in your bed?"

"I don't know."

"You don't know?"

"Maybe someone put them there?"

"Maybe someone put them there? So, you're telling me that some mysterious person came into your room, ate a bunch of candy, left the wrappers in your bed, and then disappeared?"

"I think so."

I suppose that's as good an explanation as any.

After six kids, I tend to take marker-covered walls, moldy food, and windows smeared with diaper cream in stride, but if before I had kids, someone had shown me the chaos my life would become, I'm pretty sure I would have just gotten a puppy and called it a day. Only fourteen more years until I can have company over again.

Chapter Four

You Mean the Toilet Paper Doesn't Automatically Replace Itself?

I've *decided* the reason my kids don't accomplish tasks I assign them isn't that they're lazy. I've come to the conclusion that they are simply incapable of doing certain things. I have yet to figure out a way to make them speak in a voice quieter than a jet plane taking off. This is especially true when the baby is taking a nap. And for some reason, my kids can't sit still for an hour in church, although they can sit still for twelve hours playing video games without so much as a butt cramp.

> *For some reason, my kids can't sit still for an hour in church, although they can sit still for twelve hours playing video games without so much as a butt cramp.*

I would pay money to anyone who could train my kids to brush their teeth without being reminded twenty times. Or teach them to use toothpaste while brushing. Or show them how to rinse the globs of toothpaste down the drain. Or teach them to hang their toothbrushes up when they finish using them. Okay, so they need a class on the whole toothbrushing experience.

I've spent years trying, unsuccessfully, to persuade the kids to put their clothes in the laundry basket instead of using the discarded articles as carpeting, lamp shades, doorstops, and in some cases, bungee cords.

And I would weep with joy if any of my children ever replaced the roll of toilet paper with a fresh one when they've used the last of it. When they finish a roll of toilet paper, they seem to think it was the very last roll of TP society had to offer. There couldn't possibly be another roll anywhere with which to replace the last one. After all, why should they do these things when they have a mom to do them for them?

Natural Disasters

Why, oh why, on Monday morning does my house look like a hurricane ripped through it? Looking around, you'd think we'd had a marching band over to practice outside in the mud and then invited them in for snacks, along with a half dozen sled dogs, the Bears defense, five clog dancers, ten toddlers, a horse, a dozen pigs, four coal miners, the host of *Dirty Jobs* before he'd showered, and for good measure, a goat.

It's not that my house is spotless during the week, but something happens to it on Saturday and Sunday (and school vacations)—something so extraordinary that it takes me the whole day on Monday to get it back in order.

Sometimes I wonder why I even bother. Once in a while I decide it's not worth it, and I let it go for another day or two. This always backfires. How many times has it happened that the day you decide to stay in your pajamas and do nothing around your home, a friend stops by unannounced to say hi? It's like they have messy-house radar. I can't tell you how many times I've opened my door to someone who decided to pay me an impromptu visit, only to nearly die of embarrassment because I hadn't yet showered that day or because toys were strewn about my family room or because my baby had just stripped off his clothes and was streaking past the front door naked. I've discovered it's better to at least attempt to keep my home clean, even if it doesn't really work like I think it should.

During the week, my kids do their version of cleaning in their rooms. It's not-so-much clean but at least everything is kind of shoved out of the way. You know, they put clean folded clothes under the bed where you can't see them, dirty laundry on the closet floor, and moldy old food items safely in a drawer. I'm not sure where my children learned this technique of cleaning, but they figure if you can't see an offending item, the room is clean. To that end, they make sure that anything left sitting out either gets shoved in a closet or under the bed. Ta-da! Clean!

I hate scrubbing toilets and sinks, washing windows, and cleaning marker off the walls. But in an absurd sort of way, however, I enjoy the organizing kind of cleaning. To clean a room, I have to first destroy it. I clear out all the junk that's not where it's supposed to be and scoop it into a pile. I dump out bins, drawers, and containers of toys. I clear everything from under the bed and take out everything that's been residing on the closet floor. Then I carefully make sure everything gets back to its proper home. Putting everything away where it belongs is kind of soothing: videos on the shelf, game pieces with the right game in the right box, Barbies in the doll box, Hot Wheels in the car box. Miscellaneous food, candy wrappers, old papers, and other unidentifiable junk in the trash.

I manage to get the house fairly clean most Mondays. I get it to where it no longer looks like a category-five hurricane has hit. By early afternoon it usually looks like only a small tornado has come through. And then the kids come home from school.

While I'm busy making dinner, helping with homework, or folding laundry, they are busy redecorating the family room in the classic Barroom Brawl style. When I finish what I'm doing and see the disaster that was once the family room, I generally lose it.

I begin a tirade that escalates into crazed yelling: "I spent all day cleaning in here. All day! I didn't get to do anything I wanted to do because I was busy cleaning up *your* messes! How would you like it if you cleaned your room and then I walked in and threw everything around? How do you think I feel after spending all day cleaning in here only to see you guys destroy it? Do you think you guys could ever think of someone else? You know, this is a house. A *house*, for crying out loud! Not a barnyard! Well guess what! *You're* cleaning the room now!"

Why is it that kids suddenly act all stupid when you ask them to do something? One time, Austin had been giving me all sorts of details on some video games he wanted for Christmas. He knew everything about them. Savannah had just shown me two tests she'd taken in school on which she'd received As. However, when it came to cleaning up the room, this is what I heard: "What should we do?"

"Clean it up."

"But how?" Jackson whined.

"Figure it out!" I snapped.

Lexi tried to persuade me that she couldn't clean. "I can't. It's too hard."

"I think you can find a way," I assured her.

Why is it that kids suddenly act all stupid when you ask them to do something?

Austin piped up with, "Where does this book go?"

"The same place it's been for the last ten years."

"Well, I don't know where it goes!" he insisted.

"On the bookshelf!"

Trying to escape, Savannah inquired, "Can we go now?"

"Is it clean yet?"

"I think so."

"You picked up one book. Do you see all the other stuff on the floor?" I was incredulous.

"Yeah, but I didn't get it out," Jackson insisted.

"I didn't eat your dinner, yet I cooked it for you. I didn't wear your clothes, yet I washed, dried, and folded them for you. *Clean it up!*"

Lexi said, "Okay I put two things away. Can I go now?"

Losing patience and all my sense of humor, I told them, "Yeah, you can go. You can go to bed if cleaning this one room is too hard for you!"

Meanwhile, Clay ran around creating chaos because that's

just what he does, and Brooklyn walked around with a juice box she'd grabbed off the table and squirted juice from the straw all over the place.

On the rare occasion they do actually clean their rooms, I know they're up to something.

One day Jackson came up to me and said, "Hey, Mom. I cleaned my room."

"Whaaaat?" I ask, confused.

"I cleaned up my room. Come see!" he said excitedly, pulling me by the hand toward his room.

"B-b-but I didn't even ask you to clean it," I stammered, confused and disoriented.

"I know. It needed it, so I just did it."

At this point I got wise. "Okay, what do you want?"

"What do you mean?" my son said, looking from beneath full lashes, his voice laced with innocence.

"Well, your room looks terrific," I told him, looking around with satisfaction. Maybe, just maybe he's finally learned the "It's Important to Keep a Tidy Room" lesson. Dare I hope?

As we walked out of his spotless room, he said to me, "You know, Mom, I've been reading a lot about chameleons." He continued to recite copious amounts of information on the care and feeding of chameleons, hinting to me that he'd be responsible enough to care for one. Uh-huh, no ulterior motives there.

I think, from now on, I'll just leave it messy until they're all in college.

Someone once told me that cleaning your house while you have small children is like shoveling your driveway while it's still snowing. In my house, it's more like shoveling your driveway with a teaspoon during a blizzard. But I do think there's a good message there.

I often ask myself the question "What will I remember when my kids are grown and out of the house?" Do I want to remember how clean my house was, or do I want to remember how much fun I had playing with and enjoying my kids? Although I know it's important to teach your kids that being part of a family means everyone has to pitch in and help with household chores, I think it's even more important to play with them, spend time with them, and enjoy their company (which explains the state of my living room on most days). They won't be little forever, and I want to savor every day they're in my life, even if it means they could grow vegetables in the layer of dirt on their bookshelves.

Looking for Peace, Privacy, or a Place to Pray

Of course, no matter how much you love your kids, it's important to spend a little time away from them now and then. I think that time away from your children makes you appreciate them more. I may be fooling myself, but at least it means I get a little time to myself.

This all became crystal clear to me one morning not too long ago. It started like any other morning. I reclined alone by a sandy beach. Palm trees gently swayed in the breeze. The sun shone brightly, warming my skin as I lay in a hammock, a drink with a little paper umbrella in one hand and a book written by someone other than Dr. Seuss in the other. Roberto, the cabana boy, stood over me, offering to rub lotion on my back. The sound of the surf pounding the shore was a soothing rhythm in my head. The ocean waves crashed and broke. They pounded and pounded against the shore. They pounded and pounded and pounded. *Why is the ocean so loud today?* I wondered.

I cracked open one eye and peeked out to see my kids parading through my bedroom carrying drums made from various household items: pots and pans, Tupperware bowls, a container of oatmeal with its lid off and contents slowly spilling over my carpet. Good morning, Mom!

I made my way through the toddler marching band to go to the bathroom. No sooner did I close the door than my kids started banging on it.

"Mooooom! Mooooom? Mom! Can you make us pancakes for breakfast? Mom? Are you in there? Why aren't you answering, Mom?" The barrier of a closed bathroom door means nothing to these guys.

I didn't bother to answer them. It's an ongoing experiment of mine. I'm trying to train the kids to leave me alone in the bathroom. It's only a matter of time before they will learn that I will not answer them when they bang on the door and call to me. It's been fifteen years, so any day now they're bound to catch on.

Having two minutes to pee in peace is something I took for granted B.C. Now I know the rarity, the absolute sanctity of time alone in the bathroom. Kids look at that closed bathroom door like this: Oh no! The door's closed! Mom must be stuck in there! Let's help her get out! They then commence banging on the door and turning the knob repeatedly.

This is followed by the ever-popular, long-drawn-out, "Mooooom!" They repeat it again and again until, defeated, I emerge from the bathroom.

I've learned to put on my makeup in steps. I go into the bathroom in the morning and quickly rub some lotion into my face. I leave and check on the kids before they come to find me. About a half hour later, I sneak back to the bathroom to smear some foundation on my face. Whew! So far, so good, but I don't want to push my luck and apply eyeliner. Better check on the kids. In the time it took me to put on some foundation, the kids have usually knocked over a plant, spread peanut butter on the TV, and put nail polish on the dog. This is why I don't spend too much time in the bathroom at once.

After cleaning the messes, I go back to slap on some mascara and lipstick. No sooner do I shut the door than I hear little feet plodding toward the bathroom. I stand still and am perfectly quiet, hoping they won't notice I'm in there. No dice. *Bang, bang, bang!* They've found me, and now all hope of finishing my makeup is lost.

We moms have all been there at one time or another. That's why we declare it a good day if we can manage to take a shower or do our hair and makeup before noon. Heck, I'm happy if I manage to get a shower before bedtime some days.

Take heart, though. Taking four hours to apply your makeup isn't really that bad. It could be worse. They could have barged in while you were taking a shower. There's nothing that makes you feel quite so vulnerable as your kids walking in on you while you're in the shower.

> I stand still and am perfectly quiet, hoping they won't notice I'm in there. *No dice. Bang, bang, bang! They've found me.*

Even more fun is hearing the kids screaming and fighting while you're in the middle of a shower. You know they're fighting. You hear their shouts, but what are you going to do about it? The kids know you're powerless at this point. They know our weaknesses. We're not going to come stomping out of the shower, naked, dripping wet, shampoo running into our eyes, to break up some sort of ridiculous argument. They can do pretty much whatever they want for the next ten minutes, and they know it.

It's like when the phone rings and they come running to ask us all sorts of questions. I try really hard to concentrate on the caller as I dismiss the kids with a careless wave of my hand.

"Can we have candy? Can we play video games? Can we do an experiment involving electricity, plastic wrap, and pudding? Can we have a pet giraffe?"

Distracted, I cover the mouthpiece of the phone and madly whisper out a resounding, "*Yes!* Now leave me alone for five minutes!"

They're not stupid; they know this technique works. I'd go lock myself in the bathroom with the phone (the acoustics are wonderful, by the way), but we all know that wouldn't work anyway. In addition to the endless questions, I'd also have the banging on the door.

Some days I just need a few minutes of peace and quiet to regroup. I need to hear *nothing* for a couple of minutes. I need to think, meditate, and often pray for strength and patience. Although I've yet to find the perfect hiding spot, I have identified a few places that, when used properly, give me a minute or two of sanctuary.

I can usually hide for a good two minutes if I move the shoes off the floor of my closet and sit behind the clothes rack. Another spot that often works is the attic or the crawl space. Sure, I have to lie in a prone position to fit and, sure, there are usually spiders; but beggars can't be choosers. Sometimes I can escape for a couple of minutes of solitude if I climb up onto my child's top bunk bed. My youngest children have a hard time seeing me up there, and if I pray silently and breathe quietly, I'm usually good for as long as five minutes. That is just enough time to stop, take a deep breath, and remember that my little darlings are indeed blessings and not punishments.

Some other hiding places I've thought of but haven't yet tried are the dishwasher, the clothes dryer, under the carpet, in the ficus, and hanging from the ceiling fan.

Uh-oh. I have to stop writing now. The kids have found me. . . .

Extracurricular Activities

Even though my kids aren't capable of giving me a few minutes of peace yet, I'm trying to teach them the importance of privacy. I'm attempting to teach them many things, actually, but I sometimes wonder whether anything is soaking in. Sometimes I wish I could send them to classes for the areas where I seem to be failing.

Wouldn't you just love to see a list of classes and clubs where your children could learn the things you've been trying to teach them for years? I would be thrilled to see a curriculum that includes teaching my boys to lower the toilet seat when they finish. How great would it be if these classes could teach my children to put their plates in the dishwasher after dinner or pick up their toys without being reminded two thousand times? I can just imagine the class list now!

Bathroom Basics 101: This comprehensive class is designed to teach youngsters the fine art of maintaining the bathroom. Subjects include Scrubbing the Stains off the Toilet, Chiseling Toothpaste Globs off the Sink, Achieving Streak-Free Mirrors, Dissolving Dirt, and Banishing Foul Odors. Replenishing the toilet-paper roll will be a major focus in this class. Students will also learn the importance of using the appropriate amount of toilet paper. Finally, in order to pass this class, children must learn that pencils, dolls, doughnuts, and shoes may never, under any circumstances, be flushed down the toilet.

Competitive Vacuuming: Kids learn valuable skills needed to thoroughly vacuum the house, including vacuuming both carpets and bare floors. They learn the difference between picking up a wad of candy wrappers from the floor and trying to suck it up with a vacuum. They practice what to do when a sock gets inadvertently sucked up and the vacuum starts smoking and smelling like burnt rubber. After mastering skills, children compete against one another to see how much junk they can vacuum off their bedroom floor.

> Keeping eyes open, focusing on the task at hand, and dripping into the toilet are all stressed in this class.

Ready, Set, Aim: In this class, boys are taught the fine art of aiming. Keeping eyes open, focusing on the task at hand, and dripping into the toilet are all stressed in this class. Boys are also taught how to wipe spills and drips from the toilet seat and surrounding area. Before they graduate, boys have to prove that they can both lift and lower the toilet seat appropriately.

Bed-making 101: This fun class teaches youngsters how to make a bed. Children learn that pillows should stay on the bed and never be used as weapons. They have fun while discovering that smoothing out their comforter or bedspread won't actually kill them. Strategic stuffed-animal placement while leaving sufficient room for sleeping is part of the curriculum covered in this class. And what bed-making class would be complete without learning the importance of hospital corners?

Team Tidy: Kids break into teams to quickly clean up messes left in the family room. Working together, they develop strategies to beat the opposing team in the race to clear the floor of miscellaneous clothes, books, homework, mittens, shoes, food, and toys. Bonus points are given to the team who can find the missing remote control before Dad loses his mind. The winning team gets to help the losing team finish picking up. Teams found shoving items between the couch cushions, under the chairs, or behind the TV will be disqualified.

Showering for Beginners: Children learn the art of showering for more than thirty seconds and less than sixty-five minutes. Education focuses on utilizing appropriate amounts of soap and shampoo to maximize the cleansing benefits. Children are taught that sitting on the drain in an attempt to fill the shallow shower stall with water is never a good idea and that Mom's razor is not a toy. In this class, students also practice hanging up wet towels.

Before graduating, children must prove they can walk past the steamed-up mirror without writing their names and/or drawing pictures on it.

Can you imagine having such classes available for your children? Finally, they would learn all the things they ignore when we try to teach them. And it wouldn't have to stop with them. I can see the possibilities now! This could open a whole world of continuing education classes for husbands, too!

Garbage Removal for Beginners: In this class, men are taught the basics of dumping garbage. They learn that it is not okay to walk by an overflowing garbage can without dumping the contents into the receptacle outside. They are taught that it's always better to dispose of garbage *before* the trash can overflows. Men are quizzed daily on distinguishing garbage from recyclable items and things that should not be thrown away. They are taught that dirty napkins and sticky, drippy ice cream cartons are not recyclable, but Coke cans, glass jars, and plastic containers are. They would also learn that just because they don't know where something goes does not mean it is trash.

Gift Buying for Dummies: In this beginner class geared toward the simpleminded, students are taught how to listen and watch for clues from their wives and girlfriends to help them make good gift-purchasing decisions. Men learn to mark birthdays, anniversaries, and holidays on their calendars and to utilize strategies for remembering those important dates. Time would be spent learning the importance of buying flowers and jewelry and that it is never appropriate to buy a birthday gift from a gas station on the way home from work. To pass the class, men need to demonstrate their comprehension of the fact that power tools do not make good anniversary presents.

The Theater Will Not Kill You: This class shows men that accompanying a wife or significant other to the theater will not actually cause physical pain or death. They are given exercises to help them stay awake during a performance. They are taught that actors are not football players and it is not acceptable to call out to the actors in the middle of the play. Field trips start with a jaunt to a children's theater to see a twenty-minute rendition of *Humpty Dumpty* and culminate with a performance of Puccini's *La Bohème* in Italian.

Communication 101: In this class, men are taught the very basics of communication. Time is spent on the importance of listening skills. The students learn how to turn their attention away from the television and toward the wife. They practice skills to help them stay focused on the conversation and maintain eye contact. They are taught that letting their eyes wander to another woman while they're supposed to be listening to their wife is never a good idea. A special focus is learning how to read body language. Men will come out with an understanding that asking "So when's dinner going to be ready?" or "So, what did you do all day?" is not a good idea when your wife's body language is screaming that she had a horrible day with the kids. Finally, the men learn the one and only acceptable answer to the question "Does this make me look fat?"

Hand Over the Remote and No One Gets Hurt: This important class should be required for all men. In this comprehensive class, men practice keeping their hands off the remote during a commercial without crying, shaking, pulling out their hair, or expressing other forms of withdrawal. They learn that nobody appreciates it when they change the channel at the precise moment a show becomes interesting and starts to draw you in. Consideration for the other people in the room would be stressed in this class. Men are taught the phrase "What would you like to watch, honey?" and are required to repeat it daily. Men discover that not everyone likes to learn about how swords are made, the history of war, how to differentiate the many varieties of motorcycles, or how to survive in the Kalahari Desert with only a baseball, a paper clip, and a piece of cheese. They learn that not everyone actually likes to watch baseball, football, or car racing. At the end of the class, men are required to relinquish the remote control to another member of the class without breaking out into a cold sweat or curling up in a ball and repeating, "Mommy!" again and again.

What Can I Say? She's the Baby!

When my four-year-old, Brooklyn, was a baby, she was the cutest thing you've ever seen. She had these big, brown eyes set in the face of an angel. She had cute, little rolls of baby fat on her thighs (she got those from me) and a contagious smile. She was also the crabbiest, most malcontent, unhappy baby you'll ever meet.

Now, I'm not new to this mothering thing; I have six children. I'm a self-proclaimed expert when it comes to raising kids. Actually, scratch that. I'm no expert, as the word *expert* implies a person who is very good at what they do. I'm not really an expert, but I do have fifteen years' experience in the diaper-changing arts. Had my sixth baby been my first, I'm quite certain she'd be an only child.

To be perfectly fair, she wasn't crabby twenty-four hours a day. She was only crabby when I wasn't holding her. In fact, she was the happiest, most contented baby in the world when she was in my arms. It's when I tried to put her down that she screamed. It was as if she had an on/off switch.

Put her down: Waaaaahh!
Pick her up: Silence.
Put her down: Waaaaah!
Pick her up: Silence.

She was like those creepy dolls that open their eyes when you pick them up and close their eyes when you lay them down, only it wasn't her eyes that were opening and closing—it was her mouth.

Looking back, I think it started the day she was born. She screamed her precious little head off lying in the bassinet in the hospital until I took her out and held her. Every time I dared to lay her back in the bassinet, the screaming immediately started. The nurses would come in my room and encourage me to put her down so I could get a little sleep or take a shower. Half an hour later, they'd be back, begging me to pick her up so the whole maternity ward wouldn't have to listen to her screaming anymore.

Little did I know at the time, but a bad habit was starting. Now, don't get me wrong. I loved holding and cuddling my little baby, but it was really impossible to scrub my floors, fold my laundry, or drive to the grocery store while holding a little one.

And dinner does not cook itself at my house, as much as I wish it would, so I got to chop vegetables and stir sauce while holding a squirmy infant.

And let's not even talk about the fact that after having six kids, I have precious little bladder control left. You can only cross your legs for so long before you must put down the baby and endure her screams so you can run (with your legs still crossed, of course) to the bathroom. I give many kudos to any mom who has successfully mastered the art of peeing while holding a sleeping baby on her lap. It's not as easy as it sounds!

By the time Brooklyn was eight months old, I was used to her clinginess. I carried her around in a sling so my arms were free to accomplish things during the day. Sometimes I took breaks from my work and held her so she would nap. At night, she slept with me, and as long as she could feel me next to her, she was happy. This may not be the ideal situation, but it worked for us. Let me rephrase that: I was too tired and too old to let her cry all night (I really cherish what little sleep I get!), and I was too impatient to let her cry all day; and well, let's face it . . . she had me trained.

However, everyone I know, and many people I've never met, felt the need to "fix" my baby. I would hand her to my mother and Brooklyn would instantly start screaming. "She has to be hungry," my mother would insist. My mother would take her from me at church and she would start screaming. A well-meaning member of the congregation would inform me that she must need her diaper changed. A friendly-looking woman in the checkout line at a store would smile at Brooklyn and say, "Hi." Right on cue, my baby would

> "That baby would be happier if you burped her."

start screaming. The woman would then tell me that my un-happy child must have gas. I'd think to myself, *You would know if she had gas. Believe me. The city dump doesn't smell as bad as her gas.*

I love when ~~ignorant~~ well-meaning strangers give me unsolic-ited advice. In fact, I love it so much that I always try to show my appreciation by returning the favor.

"That baby would be happier if you burped her."

"Why thank you, and you would look less fat with pants that fit better."

Or, "I think you should change your baby's diaper. She's not very happy now."

"Thank you! I think you should change your hairstyle. It's really not very flattering now."

Okay, so I don't really say those things, but I do occasion-ally think them. In all honesty, I don't mind everyone's suggestions. I know they're only trying to be helpful. But if there's one thing I've learned after having half a dozen kids, it's that they're all individuals with different tem-peraments and unique likes and dislikes and well, and to be quite honest, some are just plain difficult.

Today, my baby is four years old and is a high-maintenance preschooler with attitude to spare. I feel the need to explain to people that she's the youngest of six and, therefore, a spoiled brat. She has five older siblings who cater to her every whim, not because they love her so much, but because they'd give her just about anything to shut her up. On any given day, you can hear her brothers and sisters instructing each other: "I know it's

> "Why thank you, and you would look less fat with pants that fit better."

your iPod, but just give it to her so she'll stop screaming!" Or, "I know we've seen this movie forty-eight thousand times, but let her watch it again so she'll stop crying!" She has them wrapped around her finger.

I guess, if I were honest, I'd have to admit that she's got me pretty well wrapped around her finger as well. "You want marshmallows and Diet Coke for breakfast? Knock yourself out! You want to watch inappropriate TV shows all night instead of going to bed? Sure thing! You want to run in the street, drive my car, and play with a shotgun? You got it!"

And she talks! Oh boy, does that girl talk. I remember waiting for that moment, the moment we all wait for, the moment when our baby first learns to say "Mama." Those first "Mamas'" said by each and every one of my babies were like music to my ears. After spending hours and days and weeks trying to coax them into saying "Mama," how wonderful it was to hear this new, little person learn to talk. Watching my babies learn and develop and grow right before my very eyes is an amazing gift.

> She has five older siblings who cater to her every whim, not because they love her so much, but because they'd give her just about anything to shut her up.

Of course, those days of innocent baby babbling and cute little "Mamas" are long gone. Those first words have been replaced with nonstop talking. There are days when I seriously wonder if Brooklyn ever stops to take a breath, she talks so much. If she can't find anyone to listen to her, she doesn't mind. She just talks to her imaginary friends. Or she gets on her play phone and has lengthy conversations with nobody. Her phone conversations sound amazingly real; I've had to take her plastic Elmo phone from her and put it to my ear for a minute just to be sure she wasn't talking to an actual person. Sometimes she even gets mad and talks angrily to her imaginary friend. I should probably start saving for therapy, as I'm pretty sure it isn't a good sign when your imaginary friend gets in a fight with you.

To ensure you don't spoil the baby of the family, make sure you don't give in to her demands. Treat her just like you would every other member of your family. Don't let her cries and pleas wear you down. It's important to say what you mean and mean what you say at all times. Now, if you'll excuse me, I need to run to the store to get Brooklyn a Snickers bar for dinner while she uses my computer to play games.

Because I Said So

Kids have selective hearing. They can't help it; it's inherited. They get it from their fathers.

I'll tell my son, "You need to get your homework done right away because we're eating dinner, taking your sister to her softball game after dinner, and then meeting friends for ice cream, and we won't get home until late. So really, now is the only time you have to get it done. You'd better get started."

What my son hears is "ice cream."

As I call the kids to the kitchen table for dinner, my son, thoroughly confused, asks, "We're eating now?"

"Yes."

"Oh. Then we're going for ice cream, right?"

"No. Then we're going to your sister's ball game."

"Oh. Why didn't you tell me? When am I supposed to get my homework done?"

I'm sorry to say there is no hope of ever recovering from selective hearing if you're a male. It will continue into your adult life. You'll go from driving your mother to the nuthouse to making your wife want to hit you over the head with a blunt object.

If, by some miracle (it really would be a miracle, seeing as only eight cases of this happening have ever been reported), your children do hear what you've said and they understand what you've said and they remember what you've said, you're still not in the clear. They're still bound to ask you one important question.

> I'm sorry to say there is no hope of ever recovering from selective hearing if you're a male.

For instance, if I say, "You have to clean up your room before dinner," my kids typically reply "Why?"

I say, "You can't wear your bathing suit outside in January" my kids say, "Why?"

I say, "You need to eat some vegetables." "Why?"

There it is. The Question. *Why?*

Now when I was a kid and I asked my mom The Question, she oftentimes responded with, "Because I said so."

As a child, I thought that was the dumbest answer on earth. Really, "Because I said so"! What kind of answer is that anyway? It's not an answer. It was just a way for my mom to end the conversation, and I vowed never to say that to my own children when I grew up.

Well, let me tell you, to change my mind it only took a couple of instances of attempting to explain to my toddler why it was important to keep a tidy room. You can't talk to toddlers about a clean room. Toddlers care about clean rooms as much as they care about global economics. In a very short time, I was answering my toddlers with, "Because I said so!" It's simple, short, and to-the-point.

As we discussed earlier, they don't listen to you anyway, so why bother explaining to a child that he'll get scurvy if he doesn't eat his fruits and vegetables or that wearing a bathing suit outside in January leads to hypothermia? It just doesn't work. Why? Because I said so!

Chapter Five

· · · · · · · · ·

This Is Why I Have Gray Hair

Having kids keeps you young. You get to once again see the world through a child's eyes. If you take the time, you can view things from their innocent perspective. Because of my children, I get to play house, dress up, and pretend to work in a restaurant. I get to watch cartoons and Disney movies and take my kids places I wouldn't go to by myself, such as the museum, the aquarium, and the zoo. I get to play fun kid games and I don't look too strange doing it.

But having kids also ages you prematurely. I'm not sure how this works, but it's true. Worrying whether you're doing a good job as a mother is taxing. Worrying about your kids' development, social skills, and grades ages you. Worrying if their sibling rivalry is normal, if eating nothing but macaroni and cheese for a month will stunt their growth, or if they'll be scarred for life if they mess up at their big dance recital will certainly take years off your life.

They say the funniest things, and laughter is good for the soul. Whether they're trying to tell you a joke (*Knock knock. Who's there? Monkey butt! HaHaHa!*) or they're trying to repeat a story they heard (*God gave Eve some of Adam's ribs, but she didn't like ribs. I think because they're too messy. She ate apples instead*), they never fail to crack me up.

They also think up some of the most embarrassing things I've ever heard and usually choose to present these tidbits aloud in a public forum. One day, while I was trying on clothes in the dressing room, my son piped up with, "Mommy, your butt is really big." Approaching the altar for communion, my friend's son loudly said, "Dear God, please help me be nice and not call my brother a butthead." Little kids tell it like it is, and with complete innocence and honesty. Of course, as they get older, the things kids say don't always seem quite as cute and funny. Sometimes they make you want to shake your head; sometimes they make you roll your eyes. Other times they make you want to buy a pair of ear plugs.

And it's not just the things kids say that are crazy. They think up the strangest things to do, too. Things that would never cross a sane adult's mind. Things like tying a belt around their little brother and taking him for a walk like a dog. Or trying to ride their bike with

> Approaching the altar for communion, my friend's son loudly said, "Dear God, please help me be nice and not call my brother a butthead."

only one foot, no hands, and a blindfold. I mean, what goes through a child's mind when they come up with the idea of smearing yogurt on the TV? Why do they take all the pillows and blankets off their beds and put them out in the backyard? My kids drive me to the brink of insanity on a regular basis. There are days when I swear I can actually see my hair graying before my very eyes.

There's One in Every Family

I've been told there's one in every family. Well, my *one* is lovingly called Spaz or Monkey or Trouble or Punk. Occasionally we use his actual name, Clayton, when we can remember it.

If this kid makes it to his tenth birthday, it will be nothing less than a miracle. Heck, we had a celebration when he made it to his *fifth* birthday, not because it was his birthday, but because we were amazed he hadn't fatally injured himself. If he doesn't break his own neck by jumping off the roof, I'm sure to wring his neck for any of the numerous things he does on a daily basis. For example, I remember a particular day of mischief that happened a while back. Clayton had just turned three.

The day started much like any other. While I made lunches and got my other five kids up and ready for school, Clay used one of his favorite mediums, maple syrup, to paint a lovely fresco on the dining room wall. In an effort to redirect his energy, I gave him the job of getting me a diaper and some wipes so I could change the baby. That's a simple enough task, right? After several minutes, I came to the conclusion that Clay had gotten distracted and it could be days before he remembered to bring me a diaper, so I went to get it myself. As I opened the door to the baby's room, I saw Clay literally covered in lotion. At least it wasn't diaper cream this time. There was lotion in his hair and on his cheeks, his arms, his shirt, and his legs. The changing table, walls, carpet, and closet doors were covered. Apparently the kid really likes to smear stuff all over himself. Well, he'll have the softest skin on the planet, I decided.

I spent the better part of an hour scrubbing the walls in the baby's room. Meanwhile, Clay had moved on to bigger and better things. He went into the bathroom and, for reasons known only to him, poured a full bottle of shampoo into the bathtub. How nice. After cleaning up the lotion, I went into the bathroom to do damage control there. When Lexi walked in to use the bathroom, she discovered that Clay had also generously coated the toilet seat with shampoo and had put a whole roll of toilet paper in the bowl.

After cleaning up the bathroom, I made the kids some cinnamon toast. Stupidly, I left the tub of butter on the kitchen counter. I paid for that mistake when I heard Lexi call, "Mooom! Clay put butter on my floor!" Yes, the carpet in the girls' room was also covered in butter. Do you know how to get butter out of carpet? I don't. If you have any ideas, please give me a call!

In the time it took me to clean up (actually, *smear around* is a better term) the butter, Clay had dumped out the toy box and taken apart the girls' dollhouse. Clay just loves to take things apart. The dollhouse, the racetrack, and the play set—that took me . . . er, um . . . *Santa* five hours to put together—Clay tore apart in mere minutes. Now if only he could figure out how to get them back together again, NASA would hire him in a heartbeat.

Besides liking to take things apart, Clay also likes to pour things. He climbs onto the kitchen counters, grabs cups out of the cabinets, and fills them with water from the dispenser on the freezer door. (Apparently it's also great fun to simply depress the button and let the water run out of the freezer door and down onto the floor.) Not only does he fill cups but he also fills toys, plastic sandwich bags, the baby's car seat, cases from video tapes, and his older brother's cup (and I'm not talking about the kind of cup you drink from).

And it's not just water he uses. Oh no. He uses lotion, shampoo, jelly . . . heck, he once even grabbed a tank of gasoline for filling our lawnmower and proceeded to water the plants with it.

After lunch, I sent my youngest three off to play and sat down to do my taxes, which is not exactly my idea of fun. Personally, I'd rather chop off my foot than do my taxes, because doing taxes involves math and, really, how often in your adult life have you had to know the answer to "If a train leaves Boston at 7:30 in the morning and travels sixty miles an hour . . ."

I checked on the kids after a few minutes, only to find that Clay had scribbled on the baby's head with a pen. I washed the poor baby's forehead and thanked God that it wasn't permanent marker this time. I set the kids up with a movie and went back to my taxes. After a few minutes of quiet, I decided I'd better check on the kids because, as I've said before, quiet almost always means trouble. Quiet means something's being taken apart, colored on, poured out, broken, or otherwise destroyed.

So I got up to check on the little ones and I noticed that the baby's hands didn't look quite right. On further inspection, I saw that all her fingers on both hands were, in fact, glued together. And not with good ole Elmer's washable school glue, either. Oh no. They were superglued together! How on earth Clayton managed to not only find the superglue but open it and slather it all over the baby's hands in a matter of minutes is beyond me. We'll skip the details of the next hour, but suffice it to say, about fifty cotton balls and one whole bottle of nail polish remover later, her hands were unstuck.

This, folks, is my life. Every minute of every day. And let's not talk about the time he stole a golf cart and drove it into our camper or the time he tried to cook eggs in the microwave for fifty-five minutes and fifty-five seconds. Now I know what most of you are thinking: *This is the most neglectful mother on the planet. Does she ever watch her kids?* Some days I might be inclined to agree. It's hard not to feel like a failure when you have such industrious children.

All her fingers on both hands were glued together. And not with Elmer's washable school glue. Oh no. They were superglued together!

Let me tell you, however, Clay by himself would be a handful and a half, but with five other kids to watch, I can't possibly keep my eye on this one 24/7. For those of you out there who have a child like Clay—you know, a child whom everyone else likes to call "busy" (and I say this with as much sarcasm as I can muster)—just know that you are not alone. Believe me, you're definitely not alone. I understand. Hang in there. And perhaps buy stock in Ritalin and Clairol.

Is That a (Gasp!) Diaper?

With seven people in my family, I do a lot of laundry. It just cracks me up when my mom or sister says something like,

"Today's laundry day." Laundry *day*? They have a *day*, singular, dedicated to doing laundry? Just one *day*? I don't have laundry day; I have laundry life. I do an average of four loads a day just to keep up. After returning from a week-long camping trip, I have laundry piled waist-high throughout my laundry room. It takes me a good week to catch up.

My children are terrible at emptying their pockets before tossing their jeans in the laundry basket. Lexi is famous for leaving lip gloss and small toys in her pockets. Austin almost always has a pencil or two in his pocket. Savannah's known for scraps of paper with notes, phone numbers, and homework assignments written on them. Jackson and Clayton tend to have a very weird assortment of stuff in their pockets: rocks, gum, checkers, bugs, seeds, magnets, twigs, bottle caps, cookies . . . you get the idea.

If I'm not careful, these things sometimes end up going through the washer and dryer. Still, as bad as it is to have a collection of rocks banging around in your dryer, there are worse things to wash.

Have you ever washed a diaper? I'm not talking about a cloth diaper. Have you ever washed a disposable diaper? I have. And not just any disposable diaper, either. I'm talking about a super-mega, overnight, pull-up kind of diaper. The kind that can hold the Pacific Ocean.

One time I did this. It was a Sunday night (actually, early Monday morning), and I was sitting there waiting for my laundry to finish. Why couldn't I just go to bed and finish up the laundry in the morning? Because my son had given me his gym uniform to wash at 10:00 p.m. Yes, 10:00 p.m. Sunday night. No problem, *honey*. I have nothing else going on. I'd *love* to wash your smelly ole gym uniform in the middle of the night instead of going to sleep. I kept trying to remind myself that at least he remembered to bring it home.

Last year he repeatedly forgot to bring it home. One day, surrounded by a cloud of dust and flies, his uniform got up and walked home by itself. Giving it to me at ten at night was, at least, an improvement.

Of course I could have just let it go. I could have told him that he was out of luck and would just have to report to gym class tomorrow with a uniform so stinky his teacher would be sure to give him a failing grade if he didn't pass out first. But I remembered all too well those junior high days. It's really no fun having to change for PE in front of all your classmates. Although people told me back then that those were the best days of my life, I look back now and think those people were liars.

Kids have it hard in many ways. Think about it. They have six or seven, even eight teachers who give them homework assignments they have to keep track of. They have to do well on tests in class after class. They're expected to keep up their grades in all academic areas. And that's not all. No, kids today are pushed into participating in sports, clubs, lessons, extracurricular activities, and volunteer work. They're pulled in so many directions at once. I believe that kids today have way more pressure on them than I did when I was in school, and that's not even getting into peer pressure. And of course, in junior high, their bodies are changing, they're discovering what kind of person they want to be, and they're wanting a little more freedom. Kids have a lot on their plates.

So, saint that I am, I decided to wash Austin's uniform at the last minute so he had one less thing to worry about the next day. Of course, the next day I pulled the usual guilt trip and made sure he knew he got a freebie, but that night I thought I was doing the right thing.

I tossed his uniform in with a bunch of other stuff and kept myself busy while the cycle went through. There I was, hovering over the washing machine, waiting for it to stop so I could throw his uniform in the dryer and hit the sack.

Yes! The wash cycle was done! I opened the washer, reached in to remove the wet clothes, and what the . . . ? What *is* that? A diaper? Oh no! Oh that's wonderful. It's a supermega absorbent nighttime diaper.

Clay had a habit of taking off his jammies, nighttime diaper and all, and throwing all of it into the hamper. I'm usually quite good at the remove-the-diaper-from-the-laundry game, but this one slipped through my radar.

You know how those disposable diapers hold a fifty-five gallon drum of liquid? Right? Apparently there were fifty-six gallons of liquid in the washer, because the diaper exploded during the wash. That sticky, nasty gel stuff that makes disposable diapers so absorbent was everywhere. My washing machine and every article of clothing in there was covered with cold, wet, sticky, puffed-up, water-filled gel particles.

If you've never been so lucky as to wash a diaper before, let me tell you, this stuff doesn't come off your clothes. It doesn't come out of your washer. It stays there for an average of two and a half years.

So instead of going to bed like I should have in the first place, I ran the same load of clothes through my washer again. I figured I'd do a little writing while waiting for the load to finish. I managed to write a couple of pages by the time the machine stopped. At last, I thought. I can switch the load and get to bed. I opened the washing machine and, to my horror, saw yet another diaper, fluffy gel exploding out the sides and onto every article of clothing!

What? There were *two* diapers in the load? I cannot believe I missed two diapers! *Two!* I almost wanted to take the soggy, waterlogged diaper out and whip it across the room just to hear the satisfying *thwack* as it hit the wall. Of course I didn't. I mean, I already had enough mess to clean up without having the innards of a thoroughly saturated diaper to wipe from the ceiling, floor, and wall. Instead, defeated, I removed the diaper, tossed it in the garbage can, shook out Austin's gym uniform as best I could, threw it in the dryer, and ran the washer yet again. And again. And one more time before attempting to transfer the clothes to the dryer.

Although I know I will eventually get the majority of that nasty gel off the clothes and out of my washer, some will be left. It will live. It will stick to things. It will multiply. I've seen it happen. I will find it in the dryer now, too. And the floor. And my bed. And the refrigerator. And my car. And the backyard. And the grocery store. And probably the public library. It's an entity all its own. Believe me, I know. I've changed diapers for nearly fifteen years straight. And people wonder why I have gray hair?

Locked Out

Have you ever been locked out of your house? Have you ever been locked out of your house by your children who were still inside? Have you ever had to call the fire department to come break down your door because you were locked out while your children were still inside? I have.

Nothing makes you feel like a bad mother as much as having your city's entire fire department show up at your door to rescue your children from you.

See, my then one-and-a-half-year-old son closed the door behind me as I walked outside to dump a bag of garbage. I'm not sure, but I think I saw a glimmer of mischief in his eyes as he closed the already locked door.

You know how you can see something happen in slow motion, but you're powerless to stop it? It's like when you notice your keys are still in the ignition as you close the car door. You know you've left your keys in there; you see them dangling from the steering column. Yet, as much as you will the door to stop, it continues, in slow motion, to close. Click. You're out of luck. I think that since you noticed your keys were in the car before the door was technically latched shut, it shouldn't count, but unfortunately it doesn't work that way.

Anyway, getting locked out of the house happened many years ago when I had just a one-and-a-half-year-old, Austin, and a one-month-old, Savannah. On this particular day, I had Savannah buckled in her car seat atop the kitchen table. At one month old, where's she going to go, right? I ran outside to dump a bag of garbage—and Austin locked me out.

I tried not to panic. That worked for ten seconds. I looked through the window in the door at my son, who was standing there smiling up at me. I started flailing my arms around in a crazy game of Charades, trying to motion for him to open the door. He looked up at me and laughed. Not quite what I was going for. Again, I tried to motion for him to grab the doorknob and turn, all the while yelling through the door, "Open the door! Come on, sweetie! You can do it! Open the door for Mommy!"

He continued to stare up at me and laugh at my wild gestures and contorted faces.

My mind started racing. The baby! She's sitting on the table buckled into her car seat! What if he knocks her off the table? Do I have a spare key? I can't get to my phone to call 911! What am I going to do? Did I leave the stove on? Is that smoke I smell? Oh my gosh! My house is going to burn down! My son will be hurt! Savannah will be knocked off the table onto her head! I'm a horrible mother! How could I let this happen?

Somehow I managed to get a grip.

Austin obviously could not open the door. I had to get in. Think, think, think. I didn't have a spare key outside. I ran to my neighbor's house and used his phone to call 911. At this point, I started having a different kind of nightmare. I envisioned the firefighters hacking into my door with their axes. I just knew my son would see them and freak out and have nightmares for the rest of his life. Or maybe a firefighter would break into my house and then trip over a pile of toys and break his leg! Oh no! What if they break down the door, enter my house, and then gag upon seeing my pile of unwashed dinner dishes?

Another neighbor, witnessing my frantic pantomime, came over to see what was going on. I quickly explained. He was able to raise the window in my bathroom just enough for his son to squeeze through. The boy then walked through the house and opened my back door to let me in.

A couple of seconds later, an ambulance and a full arsenal of fire trucks and police cars showed up. A firefighter came walking around my house, ax in hand, ready to break down my door. Surprisingly, a dozen rescue vehicles parked in front of your house tends to attract all the neighbors to see what's going on. And there's nothing like an entire neighborhood gathered around a line of rescue vehicles parked at your house to make you feel like a horrible parent.

Thankfully, because of my neighbor's quick thinking, the firefighter was able to leave my door intact. Both my kids were completely fine. I had not left the stove on. My house didn't burn down. My neighbor didn't trip and break a leg over any toys while he was walking through my house, and I never went outside to dump garbage again.

There's nothing like an entire neighborhood gathered around a line of rescue vehicles parked at your house to make you feel like a horrible parent.

Well, I may have once or twice in the past twelve years, but I always made sure the door was unlocked first, that I had my cell phone in hand, and that the floor was picked up and the dishes were done. You just never know. . . .

Notme

We have some beings in our house that I've never seen. I've tried to catch a glimpse of these people, but I always miss them. I know, however, that they exist because my kids talk of them frequently.

Now I wouldn't mind extra people hanging around the house if they simply helped out a little. In fact, very often I have a few extra people hanging out at my house. On any given day, I tend to have an extra half-dozen kids or so hanging around. I assume that people think I must be running a free day care or I have so many kids of my own, I won't even notice a couple more, so they send their kids over here so they can have a break.

I don't mind extra kids at all. In fact, it's kind of nice when my children's friends come over to play, because that way I know what my kids are up to. I can be sure they aren't getting into mischief at someone else's home, and when my kids have their friends over, they aren't constantly saying, "I'm bored. What can I do? I'm bored. What can I do? I'm bored."

So it's not the extra people I mind. It's the fact that these people not only don't help but also get into more mischief than all my kids combined!

For example, I'd recently baked some chocolate chip cookies and set them on a rack to cool. When I walked through the kitchen a few minutes later, I noticed that several cookies were missing from the cooling rack. I called the kids and asked them who took the cookies. They all said, in unison, "Notme!"

Well, obviously they aren't lying to me, because they all said the same thing. Plainly, Notme was the culprit. But alas, as in every other catastrophe, Notme had disappeared without a trace.

Awhile back, I found my glasses on the floor, the frames bent and broken.

"Who was playing with my glasses?" I demanded of my children.

"Notme!" they insisted.

Not entirely believing them, I asked again, "Which one of you broke these?" as I waved my broken frames in their faces.

"Notme!" came their adamant reply.

Notme has been responsible for coloring over my oldest child's homework, unrolling whole rolls of toilet paper, and smearing lipstick on the mirror in the bathroom. Notme has drawn on the walls with markers, broken a dozen eggs on the kitchen floor, and used scissors to cut holes in Lexi's sheets. One time I found a mixture of ketchup, salad dressing, and soft soap in the bathroom sink.

"What on earth??? What *is* this mess? What were you guys thinking? Why in the world would you be making condiment soup in the bathroom sink?"

"We didn't do it, Mom."

"Oh really? Then who did?"

"Notme! Really, Mom."

I've searched high and low for Notme. After being informed that Notme pulled all the blankets and sheets off the bed, I looked in the closet and under the bed and even ran outside in an attempt to catch a glimpse of her running away. Notme is fast.

Notme is also quite artistic. She has drawn crayon pictures of dinosaurs on the kitchen cabinets and geometrical designs on the bathroom wall. Notme has pulled curtains down from my windows. (I can't even reach up that high!) I guess Notme is both tall and strong. I've seen countless science experiments gone awry, all courtesy of Notme. One of these days, I'm going to catch Notme in the act.

And Notme is not the only one who causes problems in my house. I Dunno often makes an appearance at our house as well. I can't tell you how many conversations I've had with my kids that sounded like these.

"Did you just hit your sister?"

"I Dunno."

"You don't know? Why is she crying? Who hit her?"

"I Dunno!"

Or, "Who colored on the wall, Lexi?"

"I Dunno."

"I Dunno? I think you *do* know. Who scribbled on that wall?

"I Dunno," she insists.

"Are you sure it wasn't you? It looks like your drawing."

"No! Notme!"

Notme? So, who did it? I Dunno or Notme?

It's like an Abbott and Costello routine gone bad. I usually just decide to stop the line of questioning and give up before I start getting answers of "Why," "Because," and "What." If we went there, I'd never be able to figure out who did it!

Imagine That

If my kids aren't making my hair prematurely gray, they're making me lose my mind. I realized I had definitely lost my mind recently when I found myself arguing with my son over an imaginary person.

As I walked past my daughters' bedroom door that day, I paused. Lexi was sitting on her floor, her dolls arranged around her, having a tea party. I leaned against the door frame and listened to her playing for a moment. She was talking to her imaginary friend as she poured the "tea" and served pretend cakes. I smiled to myself as I hoisted my basket of dirty clothes and made my way from her bedroom to the laundry room. As I sorted loads of clothes, I thought about how much I love the way little kids think.

Really, who but a small child could pretend that their bicycle is a race car, a box is a house, or a broom is a sword? I think it's great how kids invent their own games and change the rules to suit them. I love to watch my children play when they're imagining themselves as mermaids, crime fighters, police, bad guys, movie stars, animals, or zombies. They turn our backyard into an ocean, an amusement park, a racetrack, a stage, or a zoo.

Maybe this is why I like acting. I've been a member of my church's drama group for more than ten years. Once a month, we put on a short skit before the sermon. It's a fun way to bring the scripture home, so to speak. We take a Bible lesson and make it a little easier for the congregation to see how they can apply it to their lives today. I enjoy participating in the dramas because you get to pretend to be something you aren't, just like my kids do on a daily basis.

My musings were interrupted by Lexi screaming at the top of her lungs, "Stop it! Get off!" I poked my head in her door to see Jackson sitting amid Lexi's dolls.

"What's going on, Lexi?" I inquired.

"Mom! Jackson's sitting on Lindsay!"

Of course.

Lindsay is Lexi's imaginary friend. She's been around for years and has kept Lexi company many long days. I'm not sure what Lindsay looks like, but she seems to be a pretty nice kid. Sometimes she reads books with Lexi and sometimes she has a slumber party with her. Now and then she'll join us for dinner, but mainly she likes to hang out in Lexi's room, playing dolls and other toys with Lexi.

I decided to try to defuse the situation. "Jackson, move over and stop teasing Lexi."

"I'm not sitting on anyone," he said with mock innocence.

"Mom, make him move! He's smashing Lindsay! She can't breathe!" Lexi yelled. The poor kid seemed genuinely stressed that her good friend was going to be hurt.

Obviously, Jackson was intent on being difficult. I switched tactics.

"Oh look! Lindsay moved away from Jackson. Now she's sitting on your other side." I was proud of myself for my quick thinking until Lexi gave me a withered look.

She said in a tone that made it clear she thought I was simpleminded, "She is *not* sitting on my other side. She's sitting right there!" She indicated the spot where her imaginary friend was sitting. "And Jackson is sitting on top of her!"

Jackson was having fun tormenting his sister, so he jumped up and announced, "I'm taking Lindsay into my room!" He grabbed Lindsay's imaginary hand and dragged her off to his room.

Lexi let out a wail the likes of which you've never heard. "Stop!" she screamed after her brother.

In an attempt to bring peace, I tried once more to tell Lexi that Jackson hadn't done anything to Lindsay and she was, in fact, still sitting in Lexi's room. "Look! Lindsay escaped and came back here!"

Lexi didn't buy it. Crying, she sobbed, "But he took her away. Lindsay doesn't like him. She wants to come back here. Make him stop, Mom, so Lindsay can come back to my room."

I was a little at a loss. I mean, those parenting books don't tell you how to break up a fight over an imaginary friend.

I walked to Jackson's room, where I told him to let go of Lindsay so she could go back and play with Lexi. As the words came out of my mouth, I began to sense the

I was a little at a loss. I mean, those parenting books don't tell you how to break up a fight over an imaginary friend.

ridiculousness of the whole situation. There I was bargaining with a nine-year-old for the release of an imaginary prisoner. "Walk the imaginary friend back to Lexi's room or you'll be watching imaginary TV for the next week."

That did the trick. Lindsay returned to Lexi's room with only minor scrapes from her scuffle, and she and Lexi resumed drinking their imaginary tea. I walked away, shaking my head, wondering what my friends without kids would say if they'd witnessed that scene. Surely they would understand why my evenings end with a nice glass of wine.

Chapter Six

Yes, They're All Mine

Having a larger-than-average-size family presents many challenges. When going places, getting everyone dressed and ready takes extra time, and transporting everyone takes a bigger vehicle. Sometimes, a large family creates logistical problems when figuring out where to put everyone and which children should share a room. Parents of more than one child experience things that parents of one child don't usually encounter, like figuring out "who started it" or trying to be fair when assigning chores. Taking vacations or just going out to dinner with several children presents more challenges than it does for smaller families. Of course, over time, seasoned parents of many learn to relax a little when it comes to their kids. So, they aren't wearing matching clothes? No big deal. In the family photograph, everyone isn't smiling at the same time? Parents of large families are usually happy if everyone is just looking in the general vicinity of the camera. When their kids are crying, they don't freak out. After several kids, you learn when you really need to be concerned. "Do you have any bones sticking out? No? You're fine, go play!"

And of course there are the endless "Are they all yours?" questions and the people who think that it's their responsibility to teach you all about reproduction. "How many kids do you have? Do you know what causes that?"

"Umm yes, don't you?"

> After several kids, you learn when you really need to be concerned. "Do you have any bones sticking out? No? You're fine, go play!"

Although a large family means more loads of laundry, higher grocery bills, and more toys left on the floor; a large family also means more hugs and kisses, livelier conversation, and lots of helpers. Children in a big family learn to get along with one another, to problem-solve, and to be responsible for themselves. Children with multiple siblings always have someone around to play with or to ask for help. Despite the extra craziness, I wouldn't trade my family for anything! Well, maybe I'd trade it for a good night's sleep. . . . Nah, I wouldn't trade it for anything.

We're Not Having Chicken

Because I'm a single mom and my kids are involved in extracurricular activities, meals at my house are usually hectic affairs. I'm busy trying to get dinner ready while telling the kids to set the table, pick their belongings up off the floor, and finish their homework. One or two kids are usually whining for something, and at least another couple are fighting about something else. Although I try to encourage nice conversation around the dinner table, it doesn't generally go quite like I picture it in my mind.

I remember one particular dinner, a few years ago. I purposely recorded all our dialogue so I could blog about a typical dinner at my house. It went like this. . . .

As I dished out food and cut pieces of meat for the little kids, I attempted to start a meaningful conversation.

"What did you guys do in school today?"

"I don't like chicken," Austin announced to no one in particular.

"We're not having chicken," I assured him.

Jackson piped up, "Oh! I love chicken! I want a leg!"

I looked at Jackson, who, I guess, hadn't been paying attention, and told him, "This isn't chicken. We're having pork chops."

"I don't like pork chops," Austin informed me.

"Since when?" Apparently my son had become a vegetarian.

Savannah, who somehow just realized what we were talking about, asked, "Oh we're having chicken?"

Jackson insisted, "I get the leg!"

Do these guys listen to anything at all? I wondered. "We're not having chicken tonight."

Brooklyn joined in the conversation with "Dadadadada."

Lexi told me, "I just want milk."

Jackson, who was still clueless for some reason, told her, "You can't have milk! We're having chicken."

Not to be left out of the excitement, Clay proclaimed, "My butt itches!"

"What is that brown stuff in the rice? I don't like that," said Austin, who had turned into a picky eater overnight.

I assured him, "There's no brown stuff. Eat it." Then, trying to change the subject, I asked, "So what did you guys do in school?"

"This doesn't taste like chicken." Savannah looked at me in an accusatory way.

"It's not chicken, duh!!!" Austin barked at Savannah. Then to me, "Mom, what's 483 divided by 14?"

"I don't know, Austin. Put your homework away. It's time to eat now." Whew, thank God it was dinnertime, so I was able to successfully get out of doing math in my head.

Clay, meanwhile, was having fun bouncing up and down in his chair.

"Wheeeaaaaaaaaa!!!!" he squealed.

"Can I have a fruit snack for dinner?" Lexi asked.

I attempted to bring some sanity to the table. "No, you can't have a fruit snack. Eat some meat. Clay, settle down. Lex, tell me what you did in school. Why did you get that stamp on your hand?"

Giving up on the fruit snack, Lexi started to answer me, "We were, um, in the room, ummm . . ."

Brooklyn interrupted with, "Dadaaaa baba!" and then Savannah yelled out, "Stop kicking, Austin!!!"

Ignoring their commotion, I continued to try to talk with Lexi. "What room, Lex?"

"I'm not kicking you," Austin yelled back to Savannah.

Jackson asked, "Can I have more chicken?"

Finally I got an answer out of Lexi. "We were at school. Mrs. Wilkins, ummm, gave us stamps, ummmm, because . . . Is that corn?"

At this point I was pretty convinced that all my kids had attention deficit disorder.

"Mooom, make Austin stop kicking. He's kicking the table," complained Savannah.

"Savannah, pass the corn to Lex, please. Austin, stop kicking the table. Clay, stop drinking all your milk and eat. Why did Mrs. Wilkins give you guys stamps?"

Savannah protested, "I already have corn."

"I know you do. I asked you to pass the corn to Lex," I reiterated.

Clay gave up eating and was again bouncing around in his seat and yelling at the top of his lungs, "Twinkle, twinkle, little car!"

Brooklyn joined in the cacophony with, "Da da da!!!" as she flung a piece of bread across the table.

All the kids cracked up at the flying bread.

I tried to be stern while hiding a smirk, "Stop laughing. Don't encourage her."

Encouraged by everyone's laughter, Brooklyn launched another piece of bread while laughing. "HaHaHaHaHaHaHa!!!"

"So why did you get a stamp, Lex?"

"Ummm, because I, ummmm, was a statue," Lexi stammered.

Not quite understanding, I asked, "You were a statue? Did you play a statue game in gym?"

> Encouraged by everyone's laughter, Brooklyn launched another piece of bread while laughing.

Savannah piped up, "I didn't have gym today."

"She's talking to Lex, not you!" Austin set her straight.

"Can I be excused?" Jackson asked.

Looking at his plateful of food, I answered, "No. Finish eating."

Still working on the conversation, Lex continued, "Ummmm no, not in gym. In, ummm, Mrs. Wilkins's class. We were statues."

"Okay, you got a stamp on your hand because you were a statue in Mrs. Wilkins's class?"

"No."

Under my breath, I muttered, "I give up."

Austin kindly informed me that Savannah was chewing with her mouth open and he needed $5.00 for his field trip tomorrow.

"Oh yeah, I need an empty coffee can for a project we're doing tomorrow," Savannah added.

Still trying to get out of eating dinner, Lexi tried again: "Can I have a fruit snack?"

Brooklyn barked, "Woof woof woof," as she threw a piece of corn to the dog. Forgetting that he'd just asked to be excused, Jackson asked, "Can I have some more chicken?"

I gave up entirely on the whole idea of a pleasant dinner conversation and I snapped, "Clay, eat; Brooklyn, stop throwing food to the dog; Savannah, chew with your mouth closed; Austin, quit kicking the table; Lexi, you can't have a fruit snack; and *we're not having chicken!*"

House Devils and Street Angels

Taking my family to a restaurant is always an experience. For starters, we need to find someplace with a huge dining room so we can all fit. And then there's the ordeal of getting everyone seated with the least amount of potential for fighting, finding something appetizing for each person, and getting out of there for less than the price of a small car. It can be a good experience, though. When you get out of your regular routine, you often learn something new about the people you see every day.

For instance, one morning a couple years ago, the kids started whining from the back of the van: "We're hungry." I realized I'd lost track of time while running errands on the way home from an early service at church.

"Can't we go home and get some breakfast?"

"Aren't we finished shopping yet?"

"We're dying!"

"We haven't eaten in like four years!"

They had already exhausted the supply of old fruit snacks, crumbs, and fries in their car seats, so I decided to bargain with them. I said if they could make it through two more errands without killing one another, I would take them out to breakfast. This was greeted by much cheering from the gang.

We settled on a casual restaurant that has a variety of entrees and a sizable kids' menu. We were seated at a huge table in the middle of the restaurant in plain view of every other table. I think we were the entertainment. People looked up from their meals, their lips moving inconspicuously as they silently counted the kids while we took our seats.

The next twenty minutes were spent taking off everyone's coats, gloves, and hats and playing an impromptu game of musical chairs as I attempted to seat all the kids strategically.

"I need to sit next to Clayton so I can help him cut up his food. . . . Jackson can't sit next to Lexington or they'll fight all through brunch. . . . Don't put Clay on the end. He's too close to the next table and might bug them. . . . The high chair has to go here or it won't fit. . . . Who wants to sit next to Brooklyn?"

Finally settled, I leaned over and read off the children's menu to Lexi. "Do you want a Mickey Mouse pancake, chocolate chip pancakes, scrambled eggs, a banana waffle, or French toast with blueberries?"

"What was the second one again?"

"Chocolate chip pancakes."

"No, not that one. What was the other one?"

"Mickey Mouse pancake, chocolate chip pancakes, scrambled eggs, a banana waffle, or French toast with blueberries."

"I don't like blueberries."

"Then don't get the French toast. Or ask them to leave the blueberries off."

"I don't want French toast."

"That's fine. What *do* you want?"

"I think I want the French toast."

"You just said that you didn't want French toast."

"I don't. What was that second one?"

"Aaaauugghhh!"

"I want . . . mmmmm, I want . . . hmmmm, I want . . ."

"You think about it," I told Lexi as I turned to my other side and read the menu to Clayton, who was dipping his crayons in his water glass and coloring on his menu. After I went through the choices yet again, he replied, "I'll have macaroni and cheese."

Ugh.

"They don't have macaroni and cheese. How about a Mickey Mouse pancake?" I braced myself for the tears that I was sure would follow this horrible news.

"Okay, I'll have a pancake, but I don't want Mickey Mouse. Can I have a Buzz Lightyear pancake instead?"

"We'll see," I said, wondering what the cook would think of *that* request. I figured my son would forget about his special order by the time his meal arrived. Either that or I could practice my sculpting as I skillfully cut around the pancake to transform Mickey into Buzz Lightyear.

The waitress came by and asked if we were ready to order. I hadn't even opened my menu yet, so I sent the waitress off. I started to open the menu when Clayton handed me a dripping-wet crayon and asked me to draw him a picture of a snowman. I scribbled out a blob with a hat for my son while I bravely asked Lex if she'd decided yet.

"Mom, can I order off the adult menu?" Jackson asked.

"Maybe. What do you want?"

"I want the sweet-and-sour special."

"Can you put my shoe back on?" Clayton asked.

"Back on?" I decided I didn't want to know why it was off and crawled under the table to retrieve the misplaced shoe.

"It's on the menu, Mom," Jackson continued.

"What's on the menu?"

"The sweet-and-sour special!"

Oh yeah, the menu. The menu that I still hadn't been able to look at. "I haven't looked at my menu yet," I said as I finally opened it to the specials. "Do you really think you'll eat French toast stuffed with lemon cream and blueberries? I don't think you'll eat that, honey. Why don't you order off the kids' menu?"

"You only want the sweet-and-sour special because that's what I'm getting!" Austin complained like the earth would stop spinning if they both ordered the same meal. Savannah added her two-cents worth to the conversation. "Blueberries are disgusting," she announced.

"No, they're not! Why don't you like fruit? You're so weird." Austin defended his beloved fruit, because clearly, this was something worth fighting about. I glanced at the menu's offerings, trying to make a decision quickly as the waitress approached again.

"I want the French toast with lemon and blueberries!" Jackson insisted. "I'll eat it. Really!" he promised.

"Will you draw me a snowman, too?" Lexi begged.

"Can I have coffee?" asked Austin.

"Sure," I say sarcastically while drawing another snowman on a children's menu. "That's just what you need—caffeine." I rolled my eyes and told him to order orange juice in a coffee cup and pretend it was coffee. He wasn't amused with my clever idea.

When the waitress came by yet again to try to get our order, Lexi told her, "I'd like to have the thing with the stuff on it." The confused waitress looked at me for clarification. I just shrugged. "She'll have the thing with the stuff on it."

Clay joined in and placed his order: "I want a thing with stuff on it, too!"

> When the waitress came by to get our order, Lexi told her, "I'd like to have the thing with the stuff on it."

"Got that? That'll be two things with stuff on them."

When Jackson ordered the sweet-and-sour special, the waitress asked him, "Are you sure you can eat all that? It's pretty big."

Austin, looking at Jackson, chimed in with "Yeah, you'll never finish a Crabby Patty, Barnacle Boy." Then, to the waitress, he said, "He'll have a Pipsqueak Patty."

A good mother would know at this point that it was time to limit the kids' cartoon viewing to less than twelve hours a day. What went through my head, however, was the realization that the kids could recall every line of every *Sponge Bob* episode ever made and they could quote them with impressive accuracy, but they couldn't remember to put their dirty clothes in the hamper.

Everyone had ordered except me, so I closed my eyes, did Eeny Meeny Miney Moe, and pointed to an item on the menu.

While we waited for our food, my kids talked, drew on their menus, and finished their drinks. They constructed towers out of containers of creamer and jelly. Clayton ate a packet of butter, and Brooklyn dumped sugar on the table. Clay smiled and flirted with every waitress who passed by the table.

They're amazingly well behaved in restaurants for some reason. I'm thinking of setting up my kitchen to look like a restaurant. Maybe if I tie on an apron and hand the kids menus we could get through one meal at home without someone burping, jumping up from the table, or playing with their food. Maybe. I think it's worth a try.

As soon as the waitress arrived carrying a tray laden with our orders, Clay popped up and informed me that he had to use the bathroom. You'd think I'd have learned to order a salad or a fruit plate by now. I haven't eaten a hot meal in sixteen years.

Clay took a full ten minutes to explore every nook and cranny of the restaurant bathroom all the while I was urging him to hurry up. "Come on, Clay. It doesn't take that long to flush a toilet. Okay, Clay, you're done washing your hands now. Let's go. Our food is getting cold. No, don't pick up that garbage off the floor. Oh, ewww. Now you need to wash your hands again."

I started to sit back down, but before my butt hit the chair,

Lexi piped up to tell me that she also had to go to the bathroom. *Oh joy. Here we go again.*

Upon returning from my second excursion to the bathroom, I noticed that everyone had just about finished eating. Savannah had finished. Austin had finished. Lexi was taking her last bite. Clay was dipping his last bite of pancake into his orange juice and smearing it around his plate. Brooklyn had finished eating and was now rubbing maple syrup in her hair.

Everyone had finished but Jackson, that is. Although he'd eaten only two bites of his lemon/blueberry French toast, he insisted that he liked it and was just suddenly not hungry anymore. I made a mental note to make him order off the children's menu the next time we went out to eat.

By this time my kids were starting to get restless, so I asked the waitress to wrap my breakfast to go. So much for a meal out.

Still, I count it as a victory. Brooklyn threw only about a pound of food on the floor and she didn't hit any other patrons with her projectile pancakes of death. There was no fighting, poking, crawling under the table, blowing bubbles in their drinks, or yelling. A little old lady who'd been dining next to us walked over to our table as she was leaving and said, "I just have to tell you what a beautiful family you have. And they are *so* well behaved!"

I smiled at her, looked lovingly at my little darlings sitting there so politely, and then burst out laughing hysterically. She obviously didn't know my kids. This nice lady smiled and told me they must be House Devils and Street Angels. I'd never heard that expression before, but I like it. It fits.

Shake It Off. It's Just Blood.

A while back, Clayton ran at breakneck speed (the only speed at which a three-year-old can run) around the corner of the kitchen. He misjudged the distance between the countertop—conveniently placed at toddler level—and his noggin. He banged his head into the sharp corner of the kitchen counter, sending him into a fit of wails the likes of which you've never heard, unless of course you have a toddler who has smashed his head into the corner of your counter. I pulled him to me and hugged him, whispering, "Shhhh, it's okay," repeatedly.

After his sobs subsided, I pulled away and looked at his head to assess the damage. Blood was trickling down his head, soaking through his hair and making its way onto his face. I calmly grabbed a diaper wipe, my cleaning weapon of choice for all things including dirt, markers, spilled food, and yes, blood. After wiping up the mess in his hair, I found the cut on his head and realized that it really wasn't that bad. In fact, it had all but stopped bleeding. Being a toddler, he was finished sitting still by this point and ran off to play like nothing had ever happened.

This incident made me wonder when I ever got so calm about these things. Was I always like this? If your child's head is bleeding, shouldn't you freak out a little more? Am I a terrible mother?

The answer is no, I'm just a mom of six kids. I've experienced a lot of blood in my days.

I remembered back to when I had only two kids. My oldest son, Austin, who was one and a half at the time, was playing with his collection of large, hard-plastic animals. He threw his elephant up in the air to see if it could fly (I guess this was during his Dumbo phase). It landed on Savannah, who was two months old.

More specifically, it landed on her head. Her tiny, two-month-old, soft, newborn, little head. I handled that with the utmost calm as well. I believe I said something like, "Oh my gosh! Oh my gosh! What did you do?! Oh no! Oh no! Oh my gosh! Poor baby! I have to get her to the hospital! Should I call an ambulance? Oh no! Oh my gosh!" Yes, I think that about sums it up.

I loaded up the kids, rushed the baby to the emergency room, and explained to the doctor that my baby had suffered a horrific brain-damaging injury. The doctor pulled out a magnifying glass so he could see this terrible injury I assured him was there. The doctor, sensing my "New MOMness," sent my baby for an X-ray to make sure she was fine. Then he walked out of our cubicle and laughed his head off at me for bringing my child to the ER for a microscopic cut on her head.

Now after six kids, I've lightened up about some things and become a bit wiser in many regards. I'm pretty good at figuring out if my kids' injuries are just bruises and cuts or if they're broken bones and gashes requiring stitches. But I admit that I still don't know when to take my kids to the doctor for sickness. If I take them in, inevitably they're given a diagnosis of Snotty Nose and I'm told, "Take them home, give them juice, and they'll be fine in another day. That'll be twenty dollars." And of course, they are fine in another day and I kick myself for not waiting "just one more day."

On the other hand, if I wait that one more day *before* bringing them to the doctor, the doctor looks at me when I get there and says I'm the most neglectful mom on the planet and how could I have waited so long to bring in my child. His ears are infected and he has strep throat and his tongue is green and spotted and he has a rash on his hair and his toes are swollen five times their usual size—and how could I have not noticed that his skin was an interesting shade of chartreuse?

And it doesn't matter how sick the child is when I bring him to the office. I can guarantee she'll be even more sick approximately two days after our visit. After sitting in a waiting room with kids sneezing on books, coughing into the air, and wiping their noses on the chairs, my child will most assuredly come

If I wait before bringing them to the doctor, the doctor looks at me when I get there and says I'm the most neglectful mom on the planet.

down with something contagious after a visit to the doctor.

Either that or she'll be miraculously cured when we get to the doctor's office and I'm left stammering to the pediatrician, "Honestly, she had a fever of a hundred and five and was throwing up and couldn't move." The doctor looks at me skeptically as my child runs around the office, laughing and playing.

A great place to observe the difference between a new mom and a veteran is at a park. The new moms are the ones following their kids around, inches behind them, making sure they don't fall or get scraped or go down the slide too fast or headfirst. The veteran moms are sitting on the bench, talking with one another, keeping track of their kids out of the corners of their eyes. They're the ones who, if their kids fall, don't immediately jump up, run to their sides, brush the sand off their backs, and kiss their boo-boos repeatedly. They're the ones who, when their child flies off the slide and lands on his derrière, will say, "Uh-oh. I think you broke your butt. There's a crack in it." Of course those new moms are also the ones who can be heard talking to their children as if the kids were capable of listening and thinking like an adult. "Honey, we don't throw sand. Sand could get in someone's eyes and then it would hurt. You wouldn't want to get sand in your eyes, would you? You wouldn't want to hurt someone else's eyes with sand, would you, sweetie? Please don't throw sand, okay?"

The mom of many has learned that children are not capable of reasoning like adults and simply says, "If you throw sand again, we're leaving." The end.

It's not that I don't care if my kids get hurt. Moms want to do everything in their power to protect their little ones. But I've learned that you cannot protect your child from every scrape and scratch and it's sometimes a good idea to let go a little. Of course you want to try to keep them away from dangerous situations and protect them from getting hurt, but I think there's a fine line between protecting them and overprotecting them. You don't need to buy your baby knee pads to protect her little knees when she's learning to crawl. And you most likely don't need that invaluable little toy that changes color when you put it in the tub to measure how hot the water is. I mean, generations of parents somehow managed not to scald their children just by feeling the water before putting their babies in. It's wise to buy your children helmets and insist they wear them while bike riding or skateboarding, but I don't make my toddler wear knee pads, elbow pads, wrist braces,

> The mom of many has learned that children are not capable of reasoning like adults and simply says, "If you throw sand again, we're leaving." The end.

shoulder pads, and shin guards to ride his Big Wheel down the driveway.

I know firsthand that it's okay if your kids have bruises on their shins. One time, when my kids were at the doctor's office for physicals, I worried that the doctor would wonder if I beat my children because their shins were totally spotted with purple bruises. The doctor reassured me that he worries more about the kids without the bruised shins because they probably sit around watching TV all day instead of getting out to play. It's okay if they get a blister on their hands from swinging on the monkey bars. Don't worry about those scraped-up knees. It doesn't mean you aren't doing your job protecting your child. It just means your kid is a kid. And really, what else would you want him to be?

Who Started It?

When you have more than one child, the issue of sibling rivalry arises. When you have six kids, it's sometimes more like an all-out brawl for attention. Children compete for Mom and Dad's time and consideration. In large families, you'll probably find a couple of kids who can usually get along just fine and some combinations who just tend to rub each other the wrong way.

Although I want peace in my home and my first instinct is to try to break up and get to the bottom of any arguments between my kids, I've learned to back off and let the kids work out a solution for themselves. These are skills they need to learn. I mean, one day the child may have a boss he doesn't particularly like. He'll have to get along with him or her for the sake of his job. He can't just go into his boss's office and dump a cup of coffee over his or her head for saying something he didn't like. Well, I suppose he could, but he probably wouldn't have his job for long if he did. So, it's really important to let the kids figure out how to get along and work out their problems.

There is no way to figure out who started it when the kids argue. Do not even try. You will turn old and gray, will never come to a conclusion, and will miss several years of your life if you attempt to figure it out. The other day I made the mistake of getting involved in an argument between Savannah and Jackson.

"Moooom, he hit me!" Savannah complained.

Jackson countered with, "Well, she started it!"

"Did not!"

"Did too!"

"Why did you hit your sister? You know better than that," I asked Jackson.

"Because she started it," he reiterated.

> There is no way to figure out who started it when the kids argue. Do not even try.

"Did not!"

"Did too!"

"Huh-uh!"

"Uh-huh!" Yeah, this argument was getting somewhere.

"Okay, okay. How did she start it?" I stupidly inquired.

"She pinched me," Jackson insisted.

"I see," I said, thinking I was getting to the bottom of the problem.

"I only pinched you because you took my book," Savannah defended herself.

Unable to just leave it alone and walk away, I inquired, "Why did you take her book?"

Jackson answered, "I took her book because she called me stupid."

"You know not to call names. Why did you call him stupid?" I demanded.

"Because he is!"

"That's enough!" I said.

Savannah confessed, "I called him stupid because he came in my room and farted."

"If you have gas, go to the bathroom and take care of it. Do not go in your sister's room," I told Jackson as if he'd actually listen to my wise words.

"I only went in her room because she made fun of me," Jackson claimed.

"Why did you make fun of your brother?"

"Because he made fun of me," Savannah shouted.

"Why did you make fun of her?"

Jackson explained, "Because she took the last doughnut and wouldn't share it with me."

"Well, he said he didn't want to share the doughnut because it had girl germs," Savannah claimed.

"Did not!"

"Did too!"

At this point, I threw up my hands and left the room. As far as I know, the argument is still going on.

As silly as that argument was, I have to admit that I've been involved in even more ridiculous ones.

"Mooom, who flies faster, Harry Potter or Superman?"

"Mom! Is two plus two really five or is he teasing me?"

"Mommy! He called me a baby! I'm not a baby. Tell him I'm not a baby!"

If you repeatedly get involved in scenes like these, it will drive you to the nuthouse. There is a better way to handle the situation. When you hear the "Mooom! He hit me!"/"She started it!" dialogue, simply answer with this phrase: "Both of you go to your rooms until next week."

Yes, I know you can't really keep them in their rooms for a whole week, but it generally gets them to shut up long enough for you to escape.

Chapter Seven

How I Lost Two Hundred Pounds and Kept It Off

I knew, when I got divorced, that becoming a single mom to six kids was going to be a lot of work. I knew I'd be busy. Still, I figured it would be easier to be a single mom to six kids than a married mom to seven kids. However, I was unprepared for some of the adjustments I've had to make since becoming a single mom. There are a few things I just never imagined I'd have to do.

For example, I'm pretty sure it'll take me at least another ten years before I remember to take the garbage down to the curb on the right day. And I don't think I'll ever learn the rules of football. No matter how hard I try, it still looks like a bunch of guys jumping on one another and fighting over a ball for no apparent reason. And who knew, but apparently you're not supposed to run onto the field and yell at the kid who just tackled your son.

I guess it could cause your child to actually die from embarrassment. But watching my son's football games is pure bliss compared to tackling home improvement jobs. I seriously break out in a cold sweat if I have to set foot in a hardware store.

There's a certain feeling of accomplishment that comes when you do something like figure out how to start the lawnmower for the first time. And when you learn how to use a drill (even if you happen to drill into a pipe and flood your closet) for the first time, you feel like you can conquer the world, or at least hang up a picture frame. I've learned that I want to be *able*

> *Who knew, but apparently you're not supposed to run onto the field and yell at the kid who just tackled your son.*

to do all these "man-type" jobs, but I don't want to *have* to do them. I mean, I feel the need to have the ability to finish these tasks, but in an ideal world, I'd be perfectly happy to have a man take care of that kind of stuff while I ~~play on the computer~~ cook and clean. But until that time comes, I'll continue to learn how to navigate a hardware store and take my sons shopping for cups (and I'm not talking about the kind you drink out of).

All I Need Is a Cloning Device

As a single mom to six kids, I'm grossly outnumbered. Now thankfully, I'm a pretty laid-back person. If my house isn't spotless, I don't stress out too much. If I can't get to everything on my to-do list, I don't have a nervous breakdown. I've learned to relax about most things. But I can't manage to turn in my supermom cape quite yet. I still have this need to do everything I possibly can for my kids. I just can't bear to see disappointed looks on their faces, knowing that I'm the one who has let them down in some way. When my kids have baseball, hockey, softball, and gymnastics all at the same time, I'm determined to defy the laws of nature and be in all four places at once. Of course, this isn't possible yet. I say *yet* because my six-year-old is still working on a teleportation device. At least, that's what I think he's doing with my toaster, a shoelace, a fruit snack, two double A batteries, and a flip-flop. It's either a teleportation device or a cloning machine, and it doesn't really matter which since either one would help me out tremendously.

I refuse to admit defeat when it comes to attending my kids' sporting events. I may not be able to watch every minute of every game for every kid, but I've managed to make some modifications that help me come close. I've made a lifelike cardboard cutout of me, standing and clapping. Sometimes I drop that off at the baseball field when I have to speed across town to get to a hockey game. When my son looks up at the stands, he sees me cheering for him. I guess if he strikes out and glances up to see my cardboard double cheering and clapping, it's probably not the most supportive thing he could see, but hey, I'm doing the best I can!

I've also made it a point to make friends with the people on my kids' teams. Some days, I offer to pick up their child for practice, and other times I ask them if they can help me out by bringing my child home from practice. And still other times, I totally forget about my child sitting at the field, waiting for me to pick him up, and that's when those friends really come in handy. They can either bring my child home or at least call me and tell me how irresponsible I am and therefore remind me that I've forgotten to get him.

It's good to have friends with influence when it comes to sports, too. I've got a good friend who coordinates the cheerleaders for the football games. When it came time to assign cheer squads to the football teams, I ~~begged, pleaded, bribed~~ asked her if there was any way my daughter's squad could cheer for my son's team. Yeah, there may have been some awkward moments when a voice rang out from the sidelines, cheering, "Go Eagles! Except for Jackson who messed up my room because he's a stinky poopy brother!" I'm pretty sure that wasn't part of the original cheer. But I was willing to overlook a little sibling rivalry to avoid driving all over the world and sitting at games for six hours every Saturday.

There have been times when school orientations have overlapped, too. I've toyed with the idea of setting a tape recorder in one room while sitting in another classroom listening to the teacher. In the end, I just pick the child I like the most and attend their orientation. Kidding! Just kidding. I pick the child who gets in the least amount of trouble at school, of course, and head to their classroom.

When the school asks me to be a room mom, I have a hard time deciding which child's class I should volunteer for. What I should do is tell everyone concerned that I'm far too busy and couldn't possibly pick one child over another, but I have this disease called ICan'tSayNo Syndrome. So, whenever there's a need for volunteers, everyone knows to ask me because I can't seem to say no. Ever. I hate when I hear the words, "Sure, I'll volunteer," come out of my mouth, but I'm powerless to stop. "Sure, I'll teach Sunday school. Yes, I'll be a Brownie leader. No problem, I'd love to be football mom and take care of homecoming this fall." And honestly, doesn't *asking* someone to volunteer actually negate the whole idea of *volunteering*?

Now that I'm a single mom to six kids, you'd think people might back off a little, knowing that I'm one busy woman. But nope, that doesn't happen. In fact, I'm ~~sucked into~~ asked to fill these volunteer positions even more these days. I think I know why. It's the busy people who know how to organize and get stuff done. We busy folks don't have a choice. We have a lot on

> I hate when I hear the words, "Sure, I'll volunteer," come out of my mouth, but I'm powerless to stop.

our plates and we've become efficient at accomplishing a lot in a short amount of time. It's sink or swim, right? But I think I've found the secret to avoid being asked to help. The secret is to drop the ball and screw up everything. Yep, the next time I'm asked to fill a volunteer position, I'm going to forget to place my order in time, I won't turn in receipts, I'll lose everyone's contact information, and I won't respond to e-mails. Yep, I've got it all figured out. I'll never be asked to help with anything ever again!

Sick Days

Moms aren't allowed to get sick more than one day a year. Single moms aren't allowed to get sick ever. Really, moms can have a fever of 112, we can throw up our intestines, our hair can fall out, and we can develop purple spots on our tongues. Guess what— we still have to work! There is no calling in sick when you're a stay-at-home mom. The kids still expect you to make their lunches for school, hubby still expects dinner on the table, the PTA still expects you to tally up fund-raiser checks, and the baby still expects you to change her diaper now and then.

I had the flu last year, and I was sick. I mean really, really sick. The kind of sick where you wish you were dead so you wouldn't feel so miserable. I lay on the couch all day while my children destroyed the house. I didn't have the energy to blink, let alone get off the couch and clean up after them. I didn't have the energy to even open my mouth to tell them to stop flinging cereal around the room.

Moms aren't allowed to get sick more than one day a year. Single moms aren't allowed to get sick ever.

My middle son needed to be picked up from a birthday party, but every time I tried to stand up, the overwhelming dizziness made me fall back over. I texted my friend, Eric, and begged him to please pick up my son from his party. I whined that my temperature was over 103 and I thought I might be dying. My friend picked up my son and when he dropped him off at the house, he was greeted by the television blaring iCarly. Cereal, pillows, books, checkers, dominoes, a package of string cheese, doughnuts, fifty-thousand Barbie dolls and accessories, assorted mittens and hats, an unwound roll of toilet paper, three cups, a plate, two spoons, markers, some mysterious brown goo, and all the couch cushions were on the floor of the family room. The little kids were running around the backyard despite the fact that it was nine at night and well past their bedtime. The kids had fashioned a kind of bungee cord that stretched from the tree to the swing set and they were busily trying to do something that would necessitate a trip to the ER. The bathroom was flooded from an earlier experiment using water, soap, a toothbrush, and leftover pizza. The lights were on in every room of the house. Dishes were piled high on the kitchen table and counters. My friend surveyed the damage, then looked at me lying there like some sort of roadkill. He told me to rest and he offered to clean up and take care of my kids. I whispered out of my cracked, dry lips, "Save yourself," then I closed my eyes and fell back asleep.

Another time, when I was recovering from a bout of diverticulitis, a friend stopped by with hundreds of dollars' worth of groceries for my family since I was in too much pain and was too sick from my medicine to drive. I've always cherished my friends, but as a single mom, those friendships mean even more. A blessing that has come from divorce is that I've learned to rely on others and I've realized that I can't always do everything myself. I like to think that I'm in control and can take care of everything myself. Divorce has humbled me and made me understand that no matter how hard I try, I will never be the one in control of everything. And now, more than ever, I'm trusting in God and I'm appreciating my friends immeasurably. Now, if I could just find a friend who wouldn't mind cleaning up vomit, I'd be all set!

I Don't Think You Can Call Fifty Hours in a Van with Six Kids a Vacation

The kids and I took our first vacation as a new family of seven last summer. People who live in Chicago vacation in Wisconsin. It's the law. And that's nice because Wisconsin is less than two hours away. But did I choose a nearby destination like Wisconsin for my first vacation experience on my own with the kids? Did I choose to spend two or three days away from home? Did I start off slow and simple? Oh no, that would have been far too easy! Where's the challenge in driving two hours away and staying for two nights? Besides, I knew that a Griswold-style family vacation would give me plenty of blogging material, and I aim to please my readers. So, ~~idiot that I am~~ daring soul that I am, I chose to drive from Chicago to the Outer Banks of North Carolina. It seemed like a good idea at the time. My kids had never seen the ocean, and I hadn't been to the ocean in many years. I thought it would be a great relaxing vacation. And it would've been, too. You know, if it weren't for the fifty-plus hours spent in a car with six bored kids. Yep, you read that right. I drove there because airfare for seven people cost fifty thousand dollars. Of course, when you take into account the cost of gas, all the fast food we ate on the way there and back, and the hotel rooms on our drive down and back; and when you factor in having to clean all the bugs off my windshield and vacuuming the sand out of the carpet—enduring the nasty funk smell that can only come from six kids cooped up in a car for days—and the whole aggravation factor, I think it would've been well worth two million dollars to fly.

My plan was to leave our Chicago home at 6:00 a.m. and get an early start. Naturally, we didn't pull out of the driveway until 9:00 a.m. As I started driving, I realized there was entirely too much blood in my caffeine system, so I headed to our local Dunkin' Donuts for a large cup of coffee ensuring I'd ~~have to go to bathroom at least fourteen times before we got out of the state~~ be able to stay awake for this trip.

I headed for the tollway, but just before I could enter, Jackson cried that he'd left his camera on the picnic table in our backyard. I squealed across four lanes of traffic and headed back toward home so he could get his camera. By the time we actually entered the tollway and started toward Indiana, it was 9:45, which is almost the same as 6:00.

I had pulled up a Mapquest which directed me to drive east, then curve around through Pennsylvania and head south down to North Carolina. So, on Friday, I drove through Chicago, across Indiana, and across Ohio. Traffic was horrible as it always is in Chicago. Indiana, much like Illinois, is not a very scenic state. I think the greatest change in elevation from one end of either state to the other is five feet. But I'm happy to report that, like the commercials say, there really is more than corn in Indiana; there are also soybeans. But I didn't stop there. I continued to drive through Pennsylvania as well. I had been driving ~~a good 90 mph~~ a nice, safe speed until I got to Pennsylvania—at which point, I had to slow down drastically. I had no idea that Pennsylvania had mountains! I must've been sleeping the day we went over the topography of the United States in geography class. Remember when I said the greatest change in elevation throughout Illinois and Indiana was five feet? Yeah, well this flatlander was not used to driving in mountains. I gripped the steering wheel until my knuckles were white and my hands had contorted into an arthritic pose. In fact, three months later, my hands were still curled in a witchlike position. It didn't help that I hit Pennsylvania during rush-hour traffic. And it was raining. And there was a ton of construction. And, of course, the kids had reached their limit and had instigated WWIII in the backseats of the van. In between trying to do each other bodily harm, they complained that their ears were popping because of the elevation.

It was dark before we made it out of Pennsylvania. You know how we made it out of PA? We drove through a mountain! Yes, *through* it! There was a tunnel that went through a mountain! The kids thought it was totally cool. I, on the other hand, had visions of the mountain collapsing on us and not killing us, but trapping us in the smelly travel van for a week before we were dug out. I still shudder just picturing that scenario. I wanted to drive a few more hours to get us as close as possible, hoping that I'd have to drive only a short distance the next day. But since I had no one with whom to share the driving, I was tired and sore, and so at 10:00 p.m. I stopped for the night about halfway through Maryland.

Since there are seven of us, we require two hotel rooms to accommodate everyone. The hotel, thankfully, had adjoining rooms so we were able to be together for the night. Do you know what happens when six kids get out of the van in which they've been imprisoned for twelve straight hours? They go into orbit. Imagine one tired, achy mom trying to settle down six kids who are thankful to be able to run around, excited to be staying in a hotel, and are basically in overdrive. All I can say is, I'd like to issue a formal apology to everyone who happened to be at our hotel in Clear Spring, Maryland, on the night of July 16, 2010.

The next morning, we got up, had breakfast there in the hotel, spilled maple syrup all over the place (refer to apology above), locked ourselves out of our rooms, caused the hotel to implement a "No Kids" policy, and finally got back on the road by 9:00 a.m. Eastern time. I hate going east because of that lost hour. You wouldn't think one hour would be that big a deal, but it is.

We drove through the entire state of Virginia at a whopping ten miles an hour. Clearly, everyone in the country was driving through Virginia that day. I sat there in the van, creeping along in traffic, and watching the thermometer rise to over 100 degrees. I fantasized about abandoning my van right there on the side of the road and walking to the nearest airport. Or a hotel! There had to be a hotel nearby. I'd just tell my kids that North Carolina was closed and we'd stay at a hotel there in Virginia. I was sure my new and improved vacation plan would work!

I snapped out of my fantasy when I noticed the temperature gauge creeping up. Because we weren't moving, my van started to overheat. The way to fix an overheating vehicle, if you can't get off the road and stop, is to turn on the heater in order to pull some of the heat away from the engine. Don't ask me how I know this. All I can say is that car trouble is a prerequisite of a Meehan vacation. So there we sat in 105-degree weather with the heater blasting. If my son's noxious gas didn't kill us, I was pretty sure we were all going to pass out from the heat; and since it would take an ambulance at least three hours to get to us in that traffic, we'd all expire right there in Virginia. I glanced out the window and saw the buzzards already circling above in anticipation of our impending demise. Thankfully, Savannah was able to find a top-forty station on the radio, so we could listen to the same five songs over and over and over and over and over again while the sweltering heat turned us into a lovely fricassee.

After several hours of inching along through Virginia, we finally made it to North Carolina! According to Mapquest, this little journey should have taken us just shy of seventeen hours. After twenty-four hours of driving, we still weren't there. I think Mapquest should have a box you can click if traveling with children, it would recalculate the estimated travel time to reflect all

> If my son's noxious gas didn't kill us, I was pretty sure we were all going to pass out from the heat.

the bathroom breaks, stops for food and drinks, and pulling over to the side of the road in order to threaten to turn the car around.

As we approached the bridge that would take us to the Outer Banks, the kids, giddy with the kind of excitement that comes from nearing your destination after long, weary hours of travel, made up a new game to pass the time. They started throwing doughnut holes out the window of our van, trying to launch them into the back of the pickup truck stuck in traffic next to us. Being the good mom that I am, I made sure to ~~teach them how to aim while taking into consideration the forward motion of the vehicles~~ put a stop to that immediately. Let's just say, when the gentleman driving the pickup reached his destination, he had enough doughnut holes in the back of his truck to feed a small country.

You'd think, after all that driving, that the kids and I would plop our butts down on the beach and not move for the rest of the trip. You'd think. But no, ~~I'm stupid~~ I was determined to find fun things to do while on vacation. So, the next day, I followed some cars onto a beach because ~~I'm stupid~~ it looked like a fun way to see the ocean. I don't have four-wheel drive. ~~I'm stupid.~~ I don't have any business trying to drive a huge van in sand. Several yards down the beach, I realized my van was about to be swallowed whole by a sand monster. I tried to turn around so I could go back. That wasn't one of my more brilliant plans. I got stuck. A beach sheriff on an ATV came by, shook his head, muttered under his breath about stupid tourists who get stuck there every day, then helped us dig out. He told me to let air out of my tires. I was pretty sure letting the air out of my tires wasn't going to help me get off the beach. I think it was just his way of messing with naïve tourists who don't know how to read the signs warning them to stay off the beach unless they have a four-wheel-drive vehicle.

I changed my mind about the nice beach sheriff when it actually worked and I was able to move my van out of the rut in which I'd been stuck. He led me over the more packed areas of sand and we almost made it off the beach. Almost. Until I got stuck again. This time, it was really bad. The sheriff rolled his eyes and suggested I call a tow truck. He would've called for me, but he was busy phoning his buddies to tell them about the latest tourist to get stuck in the sand.

We finally got off the beach when a nice guy from Virginia with a big ole truck and a tow rope took pity on me as I was lying in the sand, digging away like an armadillo, and he pulled us out. My kids are never going to let me live that one down. "Hey, Mom, wanna drive on the beach today? Mom, I have an idea! Why don't you try to drive on a beach? Know what would be fun? Driving the van onto the beach!"

After the beach incident, you'd think I'd have learned my lesson and I wouldn't so much as put my key in the ignition of my van until it was time to drive back home. You'd think. But the next day, because we were all a little sunburned, I decided to drive into Kitty Hawk so the kids could see the Wright brothers museum. After a forty-five-minute drive, we got there. The kids got out of the van and complained they were hot and bored. I asked them, "Don't you want to learn about the history of aviation? The Wright brothers flew the first plane here! Isn't that exciting?!!"

"If these guys invented planes over a hundred years ago, then why did we have to drive all the way here?"

"Good point."

I snapped three pictures, used the bathroom, and we left. Fun.

But I really didn't want to return and sizzle at the beach all day again, so instead of heading back, I turned the other way and continued to drive south. I'm a fly-by-the-seat-of-my-pants kinda gal, so I was sure we could find something fun to do. My plan (yes, I'm calling it a plan, folks who fly by the seat of their pants can consider "driving that way until you find something" a plan—it's in the membership brochure) was to drive until something fun jumped out at us.

On the map, the Outer Banks looks to be about the size of an eyelash. Seriously. The string of narrow islands is tiny. It looks like you could drive from one end to the other in twenty minutes. In reality, the Outer Banks is a strip of land that stretches from Canada to Mexico. It'll take you at least a week to go from one end to the other.

> Folks who fly by the seat of their pants can consider "driving that way until you find something" a plan. It's in the membership brochure.

So I drove. And drove. And drove. And finally (after, literally, hours) we got to the Bodie Island Lighthouse. It's a lovely lighthouse, and I was looking forward to taking pictures of it. As I steered my van down the drive, the lighthouse emerged from behind the trees. It was covered in scaffolding and tarps. It was being renovated. My pictures were less than beautiful.

But I refused to be defeated. I looked at the map again and saw there was another lighthouse that, according to my expert calculations, was five minutes away. Five minutes, an hour and a half, almost the same thing. We finally made it to Hatteras, where we drove onto a ferry that took us to Ocracoke. I drove off the ferry and the kids all said, "Why are we here?"

"I don't know. I thought it would be something fun to do."

"We drove all this way for *nothing*???"

"Well, we got to listen to you guys complain and Jackson fight with Clay the whole way. That's something. And, oh look kids, horses!"

"Can we go home?"

"*Yes!*"

We finally got back to our rented beach house at ten that night. I promised the kids that we'd spend the rest of the vacation lying on the beach and doing nothing but relaxing if it killed us.

When I look back at our vacation photos, I see smiling kids playing in the ocean. I see family members happy to be spending time with one another without the distractions of everyday life. I'm flooded with memories of a wonderful vacation spent together, enjoying the beach and one another's company. Of course, that's probably just because I didn't take pictures of my van stuck on the beach, the jellyfish stings, splinters, and the sunburns my kids got—or the week-old chicken sandwich I found in my van on the way home.

Home Improvement Isn't Really an Improvement When You Do More Damage to Your House than Was There Before You Starting "Fixing" Things

I walked into the bowels of my local Home Depot the other day. Hardware stores scare me. I mean, they really *scare* me. I react like a small child walking into a store stocked with spooky Halloween decorations and scary costumes. Strangers have had to pry me, crying and screaming, off their legs as I hold on for comfort from all the scariness of the tools. Now, give me a Sephora, and I'm at home. I love most clothing stores. I can get lost for hours at a time in a craft store. I can walk into a Victoria's Secret and do just fine. Oh wait, actually scratch that. Once upon a time, I could have walked into a lingerie store and been just fine. Not anymore. Those stores that carry sizes up to a five and consider a seven "plus size" make me angry. And the pictures of the models on the walls make me want to slap them (after feeding them hot fudge sundaes, that is). But even though lingerie stores can be depressing, they're still not scary.

Hardware stores, however, are scary. I don't know where anything is. I don't know *what* anything is. Home Depot people, if you're listening, you need to have a Clueless Female section with cute little pink tools and hot guys with trays of iced mochas and mineral water for us. You can have some comfy seating and while we rest our feet and sip our beverages, the hot guys with the tool belts (heh-heh, I just had a visual) can show us the cute pink tools and tell us what they are and how to use them. Or, better yet, they can just offer to come over and fix stuff for us. I know I, for one, would find shopping there less scary in that scenario.

> Home Depot, if you're listening, you need to have a Clueless Female section with cute little pink tools and hot guys with trays of iced mochas and mineral water.

But as it is now, I walk in and freak out over the eight-hundred-foot-high ceilings and the orange aprons and the aisles of foreign-looking items. A young worker-guy saw me standing there, drooling (not because I was so overcome with excitement over the power tools, but because my brain had simply shut down when faced with the array of drill-looking things), and asked, "Ummm, can I help you, Ma'am? Please? Hello?"

So, this guy is looking at me like I'm a complete simpleton. And he's right. At least, as far as tools go. I answered him, "Um yeah, I need, um, some sort of tool thingy for drilling. Like a drill. Or something. You know, to drill stuff."

"Okay . . . so you want a drill. What will you be drilling?"

"Oh, you know, stuff." In response to the blank look on his face, I expounded: "Like I might drill a hole in a wall for a picture frame. Or use it to fill my cavity to save on dental bills."

I think I may have freaked him out with that one.

He asked some more questions to get a better idea of my drilling needs. "Will you be drilling into concrete? How much power do you need? Do you want a cordless drill? Will you be using it for long periods of time?"

"Ummm, do you have anything in pink?"

He repeated his questions again. Slowly.

"Listen, I'm recently divorced so I'm new to this whole home improvement thing. I'm not Bob Vila or Ty Pennington. (Mmmm, Ty Pennington. I just had another visual.) I just need something to hang a paper towel holder from my cabinet. I might want to hang a picture frame someday. I may even have to use it to fix the shelves in my closet. But I'm not going to build a rocking chair or a swing set or a house. I want something small and cheap, but a little more powerful than my fingernail, a butterknife, or my shoe, okay?"

If this guy thought it was tough dealing with me *today*, he should've seen me there last week with the youngest four kids running around like rabid squirrels, touching everything, jumping up onto stacks of wood, and checking out the toilet display. What, you've never heard of kids relieving themselves in a display toilet?

I tried to fix my sink the other day. It had been draining really slowly, and I was getting tired of having to scrub toothpaste rings off the sink every day. Now, I'm not completely stupid. I do have a modicum of common sense even when it comes to fix-it projects. Okay, so maybe I don't have common sense so much as I just watched a lot of TV as a kid and I remembered the old Liquid-Plumr commercials—"*I need to borrow your husband, the plumber!*"/"*No, you just need Liquid-Plumr!*"

So, I ran out to the store and got some Liquid Plumr. I followed the directions and expected the clog to disappear. It didn't work. I tried it a second time. It still didn't work. The next logical step in my mind was to take all the pipes apart and search for the Legos or Barbie shoes or whatever the kids had stuffed down the drain. I mentioned this plan to my male friend who rolled his eyes at me over the phone and told me to just clean out the stop.

"The stop?" I asked. "What the heck is the stop?"

"That little metal part that goes up and down and stops up the drain in the sink," he explained with just the slightest hint of annoyance.

"Why didn't you just say it was the little metal thingy instead of using complicated plumbing terms?" I demanded. When I was met with the dial tone, I made a mental note to be nicer to the people who offered me help out of the goodness of their hearts.

So, I headed back to the clogged sink in my bathroom with

some metal pliers and used them to tug the stop out of the sink. Well, the stop came out all right. It came out along with a piece of plastic that snapped off and went flying across the bathroom. Oops. Apparently, according to my friend, that was an incorrect use of a tool. He muttered something about the "right tool for the job" and not using pliers to break things.

With the stop out of the way, I was able to remove the clog which looked like a small chinchilla. Unfortunately, thanks to my less-than-wonderful method of removing the stop, I couldn't replace it to its rightful position in my sink. *No big deal*, I thought to myself. *Who really needs a stop anyway? It'll just get in the way the next time I have a clog, right?* The very next day, the kids stuffed a handful of cotton balls down the very open, unstopped drain. I gave up and just taped a sign over the sink that read DO NOT USE! It could've been worse, though. About a month before this incident, I pulled the sprayer completely off my kitchen sink while the water was running full blast. A geyser of water sprayed everywhere! Everything within ten yards of my kitchen sink was drenched. It looked like I'd just taken a shower right there in my kitchen. Although, come to think of it, showering in the kitchen isn't such a bad idea considering my kids recently managed to break the shower door in the bathroom.

I'm not sure how that happened. According to the kids, no one touched the door, so they have no idea how it could have possibly broken. Then again, they also insisted that the wind blew the window out of the wall, causing it to crash in a pile of broken glass on the floor, so I take what they say with a grain of salt (sometimes with lime and tequila, too). So, the shower door was magically knocked off its hinges by no fault of my children, but now I was left with the task of trying to reattach it. The hinges were completely broken; after consulting with Handy Manny and Bob the Builder, I realized it couldn't be fixed. *No problem*, I thought, *I'm nothing if not resourceful.* I bought a plastic shower curtain to hang where the door had been, but since this shower wasn't really designed for a curtain, there was no way I could hang shower rings around this thick bar where the door was supposed to go. So I used duct tape. It worked. Well, it worked for a couple days until the moisture from the shower got to the tape and the curtain slipped down. But, once again, I was right there with yet another solution. Yarn! Yes, I unwound a length a yarn from a blanket I'd been crocheting and wound it around the top of the shower and through the loops on the curtain. Voilà! Sure, my bathroom may look a little white trash even for me, but on the bright side, I didn't have to set foot back in a hardware store for this quick fix. And for those of you wondering why I didn't just call someone to install a new shower, being a single mother of six kids doesn't leave you with money for luxuries like working showers. Besides, I'm still holding out for Ty to come fix it.

Chapter Eight

My Three Sons

I think being a single mom to boys is especially challenging. I don't understand the male species, which makes communication difficult at times. For instance, I don't really know why the boys think it's hilarious when they burp and fart. Girls are embarrassed if they do these things. Boys think it's funny.

When you're a single mom to boys, you have to teach them how to do things you've never even done yourself, like shave your face, throw a football, or tie a tie. But, on the bright side, you can also make sure you teach them all the things you, as a woman, think are important for men to know. I can assure you that my sons will leave my house knowing how to cook a meal, do a load of laundry, and open a car door for a lady. Whether they'll actually *do* those things is debatable at this point, but I'll make sure they at least learn how to do them.

Play Ball!

I've never been into sports. I'm not exactly athletic. The most strenuous activity I participate in is shopping. But, like most males, my sons love sports, so I try to be supportive. My oldest and my youngest sons are baseball fanatics. No problem. I understand baseball. Two teams take turns hitting a ball and trying to get three outs on each other. Simple. And the cool thing about baseball is that it's slow moving. You can still talk to other parents in the stands without missing any of the game. When my son asks me afterward, "Did you see my triple in the fifth inning?" I can honestly answer in the affirmative. Not so with football. When my son asks me, "Did you see me sack the quarterback?" I'm at a loss. All I saw for two hours was a bunch of guys running around and piling on top of the ball and one another.

My middle son, Jackson, is the jock of the family. He loves all sports and enjoys playing different ones each season. Baseball, hockey, gymnastics, basketball, football. Ugh, football. This year he decided he wanted to play football for the first time. I knew I was in trouble before the games even began. I learned my first lesson in football when I signed him up—football is expensive. I learned my second lesson when I went to the store to get his equipment—football players wear a LOT of gear. I had no clue what I was looking for, so I quickly enlisted the help of an employee who looked like he knew all about football. He outfitted my son with all the gear he needed to play. Unfortunately, I never thought to ask the guy at the sports store to show my son how to wear all that gear.

When it was time for Jackson's first football practice, I spent nearly an hour attempting to figure out where all his pads went. There were five dozen pads in all shapes and sizes. Was I supposed to shove them in his pants? Under his shirt? In his helmet? Where on earth were all these pads supposed to go and how on earth was I supposed to get them to stay there? Some pads had snaps on them, but I couldn't find anyplace to snap them on. Even if I managed to stuff the pads in their proper position on his body, how were they going to stay there without falling down his pants and winding up in a pile around his shins? I tossed all the stupid football pads in the garbage can and grabbed a box of maxipads. I peeled the backing off the pads and stuck them on Jackson's ribs, hips, thighs, legs, and anywhere else it looked like he might need some cushioning. Okay, so I didn't really cover my son with feminine protection, but the thought did go through my mind. In the end, frustrated, I handed him the whole mess of equipment and told him to ask his coach what he was supposed to do with it.

So, I've been watching my son's games this year with very little interest. I spend my time trying to spot his number amid the jumble of boys on the field. I've had no idea what the boys were doing out there, nor have I cared. I've been content to look on in oblivion; however, the football-crazed fans in the bleachers feel this need to explain the game to me. It's not that

> I tossed all the stupid football pads in the garbage can and grabbed a box of maxipads.

I'm against painting my face and drinking beer and yelling ob-scenities at refs, but there's only so much room in my brain, and if I have to memorize football rules, then I'll probably forget my kids' names and I already have a hard enough time getting out the right name. "AuSavaJackson!"

"See Dawn, what your son did there is he broke through the line and sacked the quarterback. That means he ran past all those guys and knocked down that guy with the ball before he could pass (that means throw) it to a receiver. Did you know the term 'quarterback sack' was first used by Hall of Famer Deacon Jones? Dawn? *Dawn?*"

"I'm sorry. Did you say something?"

If you don't want to be forced to learn the game, do not let football nuts see the glazed expression in your eyes because that just makes them want to explain things to you in more detail. Instead, pretend to have a clue about what's going on. When everyone else cheers, clap! When people stand up and shout, join them! When people look puzzled and start asking each other what just happened, don't loudly shout, "Aha! See? Even football fanatics don't understand this stupid game!" I mean, look con-fused and mumble something like, "I'm not sure what just hap-pened," then look intently in the direction of the field as if you're trying to overhear what the refs are saying.

This is what I've learned so far (despite my most earnest at-tempts to ignore all the explanations). If you don't understand football and for some deranged reason, want to know what it's all about, read on.

The game is played on a field that's a hundred yards long and, hmmm, I don't really know how many yards wide it is, but it doesn't matter because the players only run back and forth across the width of the field to get drinks of Gatorade and to be slapped on the helmet and the butt by their coaches. There are white stripes every five yards that run the width of the field.

The whole idea of the game is for the team to move the ball down the length of the field. They're given four chances to move the ball ten yards. They call these chances *downs* just to make things more complicated. The white stripes give you an idea of how far they've moved the ball. Plus, they're helpful when you're trying to point out which player is your son. "He's the one standing there hugging that other player on the forty-yard line." At each end of the field are end zones. The end zones are there so the players have a place to dance after making a touchdown.

A football game is divided into four, fifteen-minute quarters, but football games last about two hours. Now, I'm not mathy, but even I know that doesn't add up. The reason is because they stop the clock every time someone drops the ball, picks up the ball, kicks the ball, looks at the ball, puts the ball down, throws the ball, runs with the ball, scores, goes out-of-bounds, gets hurt, drops a hanky on the field, wants to talk to the coach, or needs to tie his shoe. Plus there's a fifteen-minute break at halftime so the coaches can yell at the players.

During these four quarters, the players try to run with the ball until the other team jumps on them and squashes them and covers their jerseys with grass stains and mud. Sometimes they try to kick the ball until the other team jumps on them and squashes them and covers their jerseys with grass stains and mud. (There's a lot of jumping, smashing, squashing, smacking, crunching helmets, and grass stains and mud.)

A team scores by running or throwing the ball into the end zone. That's called a *touchdown*. This is followed by a little dance.

If the dance is good enough, the judges give that team an extra point. They can get points for doing other stuff, too, but it's too complicated to understand. If you see your team's score suddenly jump up by another point or two, just clap.

Sometimes players do bad things and the referees throw their hankies on the field to protest. For example, when the players all line up with their butts in the air, the goal is to not be the first person to move. It's like a game of chicken, and the first person to move gets a hanky thrown at them and then the ref moves the ball back just to tick off the guy who moved first. Sometimes players do other bad things. The ref will throw his hanky on the ground like a princess waiting for a handsome gentleman to pick it up for her. Then he'll make a bunch of gestures, signaling the player to steal third.

In the end, the team with the most points wins. And now you know as much about football as I do. I just hope my boys appreciate the fact that I sat freezing at all their games and that they overlook the fact that I asked what inning it was at the football game, told everyone my son scored a hat trick at the baseball game, and clapped when my son sacked the quarterback during his hockey game.

I Don't Have Anything to Wear

Boys and men are strange creatures. They don't care about the same things women care about. Take clothes, for instance. Men care very little about clothing. As long as they're wearing something, they're happy. In fact, they can be wearing nothing at all and be happy.

That's the difference between men and women. A man, no

matter how overweight or out of shape he may be, can look at his naked form in a mirror and admire it. He can suck in his gut and flex his biceps and he'll somehow see the image of Adonis reflected back at him. Women, on the other hand, no matter how thin and athletic they are, will see the image of a water buffalo stuffed into a bikini.

My ex-husband never cared at all what he wore on any occasion. He's been known to wear jeans and a flannel shirt to church, and he's been known to put on a nice dress shirt to change the oil in the car. I was forever buying him new clothes and instructing him to keep them "for special occasions."

"These nice shirts and khaki pants are for church or when we go out to dinner at a restaurant that doesn't have a ball pit and slides, or for funerals. Do not wear these clothes to fix the car, to mow the lawn, or to go hiking in the woods. You have a whole closet full of nasty, stained, ripped, beat-up old clothes for doing things like that," is what I would tell him.

> A man, no matter how overweight or out of shape he may be, can look at his naked form in a mirror and admire it.

What he heard, however, was the teacher from the old Charlie Brown cartoons. "Wah wah wah-wah. Wah-wah wah wah wah." At least, I'm pretty sure that's what he heard, because inevitably, I'd find him out in the garage the next day, welding, while wearing his new dress shirt, oblivious to the little flying sparks igniting the sleeves.

Not only do they not care about their own clothes, but men also don't care much about anyone else's clothes. If you're fortunate enough to have a husband who is willing to help out, you surely know what I'm talking about here. The kids get in the car, ready for church, wearing Christmas sweaters, shorts, black socks, and sandals in July.

"Let me guess. Dad helped you get dressed?"

They also do not understand the following statement: "I have nothing to wear." If you have clothes in your closet, you have something to wear, according to the law of man. They don't get it when you say, "I can't wear that because I wore it last week." Or, "These pants are all too small for me, so I can't wear them."

"If they're too small, why don't you give them away?"

"Because they're too small *right now*. I'm going to wear them again when I lose a little weight."

"What about that dress?"

"I can't wear that! It's too dressy!"

"What's wrong with those shoes?"

"I can only wear those when I won't be doing a lot of standing, because they make my feet hurt.

"If they make your feet hurt, why don't you get rid of them?"

"Because they look so great!"

"Well, how about this shirt?"

"You can't be serious! I can't wear a pumpkin-colored shirt in spring. That's a fall shirt!

"This?"

"Too casual."

"This?"

"Out of style."

"This?"

"It makes me look fat."

"This?"

"I don't like that one."

"This?"

"I can't wear that. It isn't Memorial Day yet."

Somewhere along the way, your words were replaced with "Wah wah wah-wah. Wah-wah wah wah wah," in your husband's ears.

When my oldest son went to his first school dance last year, I was at a loss. I'd never gone shopping for suits and ties. I had no idea where to even begin. I was used to shopping for my daughters. I'd perfected the, "I don't care what your friends are wearing; you can't wear that dress because it's completely inappropriate" speech. I was an expert at shopping for girls' clothing. But suits? Ties? What's the difference between a sport coat and a suit? What should he wear to the dance? What colors go together? Should they match? Contrast? I had no clue.

I walked into the store with my teenage son and started looking at dress shirts. Why did they all have two sizes on them? Why on earth are there two numbers? I threw my hands up in the air and found a salesman. He whipped out a handy tape measure and measured Austin's arm and neck. The two numbers on the shirt pertained to arm length and neck circumference. Neck circumference! How crazy is that? You don't shop for women's clothing like that. I've never had to measure my neck in order to buy a shirt.

But I soon discovered that shopping for his formal attire was a piece of cake. On the night of the dance, I realized I'd never tied a tie before. Neither had my son.

"Just hold still. I've almost got it," I instructed Austin.

"You're choking me! This does not look right," Austin complained.

I stepped back to admire my handiwork. I tilted my head to the side and squinted.

"Well, it's in a knot," I finally said.

"Yeah, it looks fabulous if you're trying to make it look like you're tying a boat to the dock," my son said, sarcastically.

I had to admit he was right, although I personally thought it looked more like a couple of snakes entwined than a mooring line. Either way, I couldn't let him leave the house like that, so I ran to my computer and quickly downloaded some instructional videos on tying a necktie. Armed with my newfound knowledge, I made a brave second attempt at Austin's tie. Then I made a third attempt. Then a fourth. After the thirty-second try, I gave up and marched my son across the street to my neighbor's house and begged him to fix Austin's tie so it wouldn't look like a hangman's noose or a dog collar.

I'm buying him a clip-on for prom.

Boys Are Insane

The differences between men and women are astounding. One isn't better than the other; they're simply different. I've tried to understand men. Really, I have. Unfortunately, I just can't. I really can't begin to understand what makes the male species tick. I do know, however, that the differences between men and women begin at birth.

My sons (yes, pretty much all three of them) are insane. I do not understand boys. I do not pretend to understand boys. I honestly do not have a clue when it comes to boys and their unpredictable behavior. They say women are from Venus and men are from Mars. I beg to differ. Men aren't from Mars. Men are from a land where creative name calling is revered, an attention span of fifteen seconds is expected, and bodily functions are always hilarious.

I began to suspect these differences were innate when I took my firstborn son to the pediatrician's office for his first checkup. No sooner did the doctor remove his diaper than my newborn peed all over him. Although I was embarrassed, I could see a distinctly proud glint in his father's eyes. "Did you see that arc? He got some serious distance there!" he said. "That's my boy!" This should have clued me in to what lay ahead.

His reaction to the projectile-urine incident was just proof that the male's appreciation of such doesn't change with age. It doesn't matter whether they're two, eight, or thirty-seven, bodily functions *always* amuse. Although a little girl would be embarrassed if she passed gas, boys of all ages are actually proud when their toxic flatulence knocks over the dog. In fact, they compete with one another in the disgusting arts. They try to outburp each other, because really, who wouldn't want to taste their dinner all over again? Burping the alphabet is a milestone all boys are expected to hit by the time they're seven years old. Clearing a room with a gaseous assault on the olfactory senses that kills houseplants is a talent that receives high praise from other men. And a man just wouldn't be a man if he couldn't write his name in the snow. In yellow. Liquid. I think you know what I'm talking about.

Another feat of great talent is achieving maximum

> Clearing a room with a gaseous assault on the olfactory senses that kills houseplants is a talent that receives high praise from other men.

velocity when hocking up a glob of spit. The man who can spit and then catch it back in his mouth does not, oddly enough, cause nausea in fellow men. Oh no, he receives applause for his athletic spitting ability.

It isn't just the ability to break wind in creative ways that sets apart boys. Boys are just plain crazy. I'm quite certain of it. How else would you explain the following scene?

My then-three-year-old Clayton ran into the room at sixty miles per hour, wearing underwear, a cape, and cowboy boots; stopped dead in his tracks; shouted out, "Chicken nugget!" and then turned and charged into the wall headfirst, finally falling backward and laughing. This was followed by the same three-year-old getting up and spinning in circles while yelling, "Poop! You poop on your head! Poop! Poop! *Poopy!*"

He then got dizzy, staggered toward his brother, smacked him on the back and demanded, "Read me a book!" His brother, being a boy of equal craziness, picked up the three-year-old, lifted him over his shoulders, and yelled, "How would you like to fly, Monkey Boy?" as he threw him onto the couch and proceeded to sit on him. At this point, the third brother, also crazy, piped up and chanted, "Fart on him! Fart on him! Fart on him!" The three-year-old scrambled loose, stuck out his tongue at his brothers, and let loose a battle cry as he ran through the house while pillows, launched by his brothers, whizzed by him. He ran up to my sister, who had no kids at the time, and stated, "My butt itches," and then he disappeared into his room. Boys are crazy.

You don't see girls acting like that. When presented with a doll, a girl will dress it, wrap it in a blanket, and pretend to feed it. Girls are nurturing, caring, compassionate. A boy, on the other hand, will sword-fight with the doll and then swing its decapitated head around by its hair while laughing hysterically. That's just how boys work.

When asked their opinion on something, boys tell you exactly what they're thinking, without a second thought about anyone's feelings. "Dinner tastes gross!" The fact that you slaved away cooking over a hot stove for an hour means nothing to a boy. They just don't get the finer art of trying to spare another's hurt feelings. This is why men, when confronted with the question, "Does this make me look fat?" will answer with, "Well, yeah, it kinda does."

While girls draw pictures of furry animals, hearts, smiling people, and rainbows in bright colors, boys draw things like blood, gore, death, and destruction all in black and gray with the occasional spurt of red crayon for blood.

Boys think they're invincible. Maybe it stems from all the superheroes they idolize, but somewhere along the line, boys get the idea that they can do anything. They don't hesitate to jump off the garage roof to prove to their buddies they can do it. They think it's a great idea to skateboard on a metal rail down a set of concrete stairs. Why do you think there are so many videos of boys injuring themselves in stupid ways on *America's Funniest Home Videos?* Because boys are crazy.

When boys get in a fight with their buddies, they punch each other a couple of times, call each other names, and end with, "Hey, you wanna play some baseball?" The buddy agrees and the fight is entirely forgotten. The end.

Who functions like that? I can't comprehend this sort of fighting. How can they not remain enemies for weeks? How can they make up a mere five minutes after they started the fight? How can they not come back in a month and bring up the fight again? What goes on in the head of a boy?

Boys do not care one little bit about clothes. They shed their clothes on the floors of their rooms when they go to bed. In the morning, they retrieve the same clothes and proceed to dress. They can wear the same T-shirt for three and a half weeks without noticing any unseemly odors emanating from it. They bust through the knees of their jeans the first time they put them on. One time my son took a pair of scissors and purposely cut through all the stitching on his tennis shoes. He sat in class, just working away on these shoes, until there were gaping holes along the top and sides. Then, because they weren't quite bad enough, he separated the rubber soles from the upper part of the shoes. Seriously. He used his ruler and kept working it back and forth until each sole was connected by only a thin thread at the heel. Why? Why do they do things like this? Why? I was not about to go buy him a new pair of shoes for that little trick, so he wore these ripped up, air-conditioned, soleless shoes for the rest of the school year. My daughters would never dream of harming one of their precious shoes.

Boys also think that combing one's hair or brushing one's teeth is a biannual affair, and their idea of putting on deodorant leaves something to be desired. I think my oldest son brushed his teeth five times last year. On the bright side, if this keeps up, I guess I won't have to worry about dating any time soon.

Boys carpet their rooms with dirty laundry and furnish their shelves with dust and empty dishes. My sons like to collect things, too. It's not uncommon for me to find empty toilet-paper rolls, assorted gum wrappers, apple cores, and/or empty bottles of soft soap. Assorted wildlife live under their beds, and their beds look like they've been slept in by a family of tree sloths. Their rooms always smell like dirty diapers, feet, and boiled cabbage.

Boys' conversations consist of "Huh," "I dunno," "What," and "Yeah."

"Do you have any homework tonight?"

"Huh?"

"I said, do you have any homework?"

"I dunno."

"What do you mean 'I dunno'?"

"What?"

"Ugh! Do. You. Have. Any. Homework. To. Do. Tonight?"

"Yeah."

"Did you brush your teeth?"

"Huh?"

"Did you brush your teeth yet?"

"I dunno."

"Go brush your teeth!"

"What?"

"Will you just go brush your teeth already?!"

"Yeah."

Some people say that caregivers are the ones responsible for programming a boy or girl to act in certain gender-specific ways. All I can say is, "You obviously don't have both boys and girls." This stuff isn't taught. Boys are born insane and it just progresses into adulthood. If we could teach our boys how to behave differently, don't you think there would be scores of well-mannered, polite, nonburping, doll-playing, rainbow-coloring, hygiene-oriented, well-clothed guys out there?

I guess somewhere along the line, women become insane, too. How else can you explain the fact that they somehow manage to fall in love with these guys?

Chapter Nine

The Reason I Haven't Quit (Yet)

More often than not, I have days that are trying, kids who test my patience, and an endless list of chores that I never seem to finish. I have laundry that is never quite done, dishes piled up, bathrooms that need to be cleaned, carpets that need to be vacuumed, and dinners that need to be cooked. For some reason, my children have this idea that they should eat every single day. I can never keep food in the house and am constantly running out to the grocery store. I have a hard time making sure the bills are paid and the kids all have clothes that fit them. I often forget to leave my kids lunch money or to RSVP to birthday-party invitations. I usually feel like I'm not a very good mother and I wish I could do a better job. I'm almost never thanked for any of the things I do on a daily basis. So why do I keep doing it?

I do it for the smile Brooklyn gives me every morning; that smile that lights up her eyes and says she loves me whether the floors are clean or not. I do it for Jackson, who makes me laugh when he tells me his plans to invent some marvelous machine that will clean his room for him. I do it for Savannah when she comes to me with a problem, completely trusting that I have all the answers. I do it for Austin, who looks to me for reassurance that he's doing all right. I do it for Lexi, who takes my hand and pulls me into her room to play a game with her. I do it for Clay, who brings me a book, climbs into my lap, and looks up at me expectantly as I start to read his favorite story.

I'm almost never thanked for any of the things I do on a daily basis. So why do I keep doing it?

Occasionally, one of my children demonstrates that they're learning some of the things I've tried so hard to teach them. For instance, one night Jackson was jumping around the room, being loud and goofy because this is what kids do at night. They save up that last little burst of energy and use it just when we've officially run out of steam. They catch you off guard this way. I warned him that he either needed to settle down or go to bed. He chose to go into orbit, so I sent him to bed.

"But, Mom, can't I have a second chance?"

"No. You made your choice, now get in bed."

"Pleeeeease can I have a second chance?"

"This is non-negotiable. Good night."

"But Mom, God gives second chances."

Now how am I supposed to answer that?! Eventually, I just stammered, "That's very true, honey. God does give second chances. But I'm not God. Now go to bed." When one of my kids actually learns something, it makes it all worthwhile. Of course, as much as I'd like to take credit for his learning, it was Bob and Larry in the VeggieTales *Jonah* movie, who are to blame . . . er, I mean, who taught him that one.

But still, it shows me that there is hope for them, after all. They can be taught. Maybe enough of these little lessons are sinking in and they'll turn out to be well-adjusted, honorable members of society despite the fact that as I write this, the little ones are smearing bananas in their hair.

This is the important stuff. This is the stuff I'll remember when I'm old and gray(er). This is why I haven't quit. Well, that and the fact that I'm pretty sure there's no one else who would be willing to take my place!

You Can't Be Talking About My Son

Just last week, I went to my child's parent/teacher conference at school. I walked in, shook the teacher's hand, and nervously sat down, preparing to hear what an awful child I had and how he was impossible to manage and, well, what kind of parent was I, anyway?

"Hello, Mrs. Meehan," the teacher said cheerfully. "Austin is such a bright child. He's doing extremely well this year. He had the highest score on the fall reading test and he's gotten As on all his homework thus far. I'm very pleased with the amount of time he's spent reading this semester."

That's all it took to get me beaming from ear to ear. *My child is doing well*, I thought to myself! I nearly dislocated my shoulder patting myself on the back. I envisioned the stunning gown I would wear while I made my acceptance speech as I was handed the Mother of the Year award. My eyes glazed as I stared off, imagining the crowd cheering for me.

I broke out of my reverie as the teacher continued with "He's very helpful around the classroom. Most of the time I don't even need to ask for assistance. He just volunteers."

Amazing, I thought. *He's really helpful at school? That's just wonderful!* I couldn't have smiled any brighter because, of course, it was my wonderful parenting that prepared him to be such a superb student and all-around awesome human being. I drifted back to my vision of the Mother of the Year awards. Fireworks lit up the stage, spelling out my name in sparkling, multicolored letters.

"He keeps his desk neat and organized, he completes all his assignments on time, and he works quietly by himself and never disturbs his classmates."

This is the point where I realize she's talking about the wrong child. I picture myself in tattered rags as the Mother of the Year people snatch the trophy away from my clutching hands.

I interrupt. "Excuse me. I'm sorry, but you're talking about the wrong child. My son is Austin. Austin Meehan."

"Oh, I *am* talking about Austin. He's doing wonderfully this year. He's a joy to have in class," she insists. "We've started a new program this year that rewards students for exhibiting exceptional character. He was this classroom's first recipient of the reward because he gave up his recess to stay in and help another student with some math work. Austin is very good at math."

"Really, you have the wrong child. My son couldn't possibly have a neat and organized desk. His bedroom is a biohazard. You need a hard hat and a bulldozer to get into it. And I can't imagine my son being helpful at school. He acts like I'm sticking bamboo under his fingernails if I ask him to put his dirty clothes in the hamper at home. Seriously, you'd think I was stabbing him in the eye with shards of glass judging by his reaction when I ask him to put his plate in the dishwasher." I shook my head. "And furthermore, I'm quite certain my son has never done anything quietly in his life. There is no way I can imagine Austin giving up his recess to help someone else. The Austin I know would stab his siblings' hands with a fork to get the last pancake. The Austin I know would lie around in his pajamas and play video games all day if I let him."

The teacher looked at me as if I had two heads. She obviously thought I didn't know my own child and reiterated that he was a wonderful addition to her class this year. I got up numbly and left that conference shaking my head. I drove home wondering where I'd gone wrong.

Obviously he could behave like a human being for his teacher. Why couldn't he act like that at home? When I reached home, I walked to the disaster area that is my son's room and informed him that his teacher was moving in with us.

"Really, you have the wrong child. My son couldn't possibly have a neat and organized desk. His bedroom is a biohazard."

Mother's Day

I'm not a morning person. In fact, I've never been a morning person. I used to drive my mother insane each and every morning when I was a kid. My mom was and still is a morning person. You know the type: they jump out of bed happily humming along with the birds, make their bed, shower, dress, cook breakfast, read the paper, discover life on another planet, and invent a car that runs on mud all before 5:00 a.m. This is my mom. I, on the other hand, am the kind of person who hits the snooze button on the alarm clock fifty-three times before throwing the clock against the wall, pulling the covers up around my head, and falling back asleep.

I can stay up until three in the morning without blinking an eye, but when 7:00 a.m. rolls around, I still play the snooze-alarm game on a daily basis. My children, however, are small versions of my mother, who delight in waking me up by running through the house, shrieking the bloodcurdling screams of a bad actor in a horror movie. It's a great way to start the day.

Once a year, however, I get to sleep in peace. That's on Mother's Day. I remember a particular Mother's Day a few years ago. I had five children at the time. After a particularly bad week of the kids waking up super early and being super crazy in the morning, they surprised me that Mother's Day by letting me sleep until nine! I awoke to my two oldest children bringing me breakfast in bed. I was certain that either (a) I was in the Twilight Zone and those were not my children but cyborgs programmed to cook *or* (b) I was on *Candid Camera*.

They came in my room carrying a cookie sheet as a tray. On the cookie sheet was a stack of pancakes with syrup, a plate of toast with jelly, and a glass of orange juice. Wow! After being reassured that the two kids bringing me my breakfast were indeed my children and not aliens who'd taken over their bodies, I took a bite of the pancakes, only to discover that they weren't actually pancakes. I'm not certain what they were, but they were definitely not pancakes.

First, they were black, and I'm pretty sure I've never seen pancakes quite this shade at IHOP. Second, we were out of eggs. How did they make pancakes without eggs? And last, what were they doing using the stove? I thank God they didn't injure themselves or burn down the house.

After being reassured that the two kids bringing me my breakfast were indeed my children and not aliens who'd taken over their bodies, I took a bite of the pancakes, only to discover that they weren't actually pancakes.

What were the other three children doing while my oldest two were playing Emeril in the kitchen? Well, two of them were watching a movie. And Clay was sitting in his high chair eating the breakfast that my two oldest had prepared for him. It was a breakfast of pineapple. Yep, that's it. Just pineapple. A whole big can of pineapple. It was so thoughtful of my oldest kids to help out and give the baby breakfast that I just didn't have the heart to tell them they had given the baby enough citric acid to last a year and a half. The baby's poor little butt burst into flames every time he pooped for the next two days. I don't think I've ever used so much diaper cream in my life. Still, it was a wonderful gesture on my kids' part. So wonderful, in fact, that I hardly noticed the pancake batter splattered all over the stove and the orange juice spilled on the floor and the jelly on the countertops and the bread in the open bag sitting on the counter drying out. Hardly.

My breakfast in bed was followed by opening gifts from my kids. I received the most wonderful Mother's Day presents from my children. Austin had made me a very cool candleholder out of a clay pot. Who knew you could make a candleholder out of a pot? Now I can do something useful with all the pots I stacked in my garage after I killed the plants that were once housed in them. On second thought, that's a little too Martha Stewart for me. I'm more of a "throw away your old junk" person rather than a "make a lovely centerpiece using only an old diaper, pipe cleaners, and gold spray paint" person.

Savannah gave me a magnet made from a ceramic tile. Where do teachers come up with these creative ideas? She drew a picture of a rainbow and a heart on it.

At school, Jackson made me a pretty bracelet. He used pink and purple beads because "girls like pink and purple." It also had some beads that spelled out M O M and I was informed by my son that two beads on the bracelet were actual diamonds. Wow, that must have blown the kindergarten budget for the year.

And Lexington gave me a beautiful, fragrant bouquet of the most lovely, bright yellow flowers: hand-picked dandelions.

Although I baked, did dishes and laundry, and took care of the kiddos as always, it was a wonderful day. The kids only fought half as much as usual, and my husband had my car washed for me, and that's all good in my book.

In the end, I choked down every last bite of that breakfast, because that's what moms do. We appreciate all the little things our kids do for us, from the burnt, chewy pancake breakfasts to the homemade Mother's Day cards, to the mud pies and sloppy kisses.

I have some more of the most wonderful homemade gifts from

my kids that I will save forever. I'll pull them out one day and fondly remember how absolutely wonderful my kids are. I'll reflect on how they were perfect little angels growing up. (Hey, it's my fantasy! I can have a selective memory if I want to!)

Parenting 101

My kids are each unique individuals. No two of them are the same. It amazes me how children from the same family, raised in the same house, with the same set of rules, can turn out so differently.

Austin, given the opportunity, would draw and do art projects all day long. Jackson would spend his free time writing or playing video games. Savannah would opt to hang out with her friends. Lexi would happily spend her free time playing with her dolls, and Clay and Brooklyn would drag out every toy they own and surround themselves with the mess.

Austin didn't sleep through the night until he was almost eighteen months old. Savannah threw up every time I fed her when she was an infant. Jackson was a happy, easygoing baby, and when Lexi was younger, she loved to sing and put on shows for everyone. Clayton has always cracked us up with his silliness. And Brooklyn has a stubborn streak a mile wide.

When I announce it's time for bed, every one of my kids has a different reaction. Brooklyn gives me a scornful look and loudly disagrees. "No!" Clayton runs around the house thinking that he won't have to go to bed if I can't catch him. And every night, without fail, he says that same thing: "Will you tuck me in, Mom?"

"Yes, I'll tuck you in, just like I do every night."

I go into his room and kiss him good night and he kisses my nose and my right eye. I have no idea why he does this, but he does it every night. Then he says, "Will you leave my door open?" He asks me this every single night, like I'm going to suddenly forget the routine and close his door.

Lexi gets up and brushes her teeth, asking only for a bedtime story. Of course, she sits in her bed playing quietly with her dolls for hours if I don't go back to her room half a dozen times and remind her to go to sleep.

When Savannah is told to go to bed, she gives me a kiss good night and goes to bed.

When Austin is told that it's bedtime, he acts like he didn't hear. He continues to sit on the couch watching TV, thinking that somehow I won't notice he's still there. This can go on for twenty minutes while I repeat myself.

And when Jackson is told to get to bed, he suddenly develops some horrible life-threatening condition for which he must stay up. "But my elbow hurts. My eyebrows ache. I think there's something wrong with my nose because I can't wiggle it." When I don't buy in to his ailments, he switches tactics and starts the stalling game, getting out of bed every five minutes. "I'm just getting some water. I just have to go to the bathroom. I just remembered I have to do some homework. Can I have a cheeseburger for a snack?"

Each of my kids is an individual, a gift from God. They are each very different and I'm so blessed to have been given the opportunity to raise six

"But my elbow hurts. My eyebrows ache. I think there's something wrong with my nose because I can't wiggle it."

wonderful children. I'm not sure what God was thinking when He entrusted these precious little souls to me, as I'm pretty sure I've screwed up one or two of them already, but I figure He knows what He's doing (which makes one of us).

Parents of young children are tested daily. Since babies don't come with owner's manuals (and let's face it, how many people would really read them anyway?), we have to figure things out as we go along. We can read books written by "experts." We can take childrearing classes. Videos are available on breastfeeding, potty training, disciplining, teaching, playing with, nurturing, and caring for your young child. We can watch special reports on TV. We can ask our pediatricians and other doctors.

But when it comes right down to it, we're the *real* experts. We know our children better than any so-called expert out there. We know that each of our children is different and unique. We know that no two children are alike and no one form of discipline works the same for every child. Besides, what parenting book can tell you what to do when your child climbs on top of the refrigerator, eats staples, and dyes the dog's fur blue? What other expert knows how you can stop your young one from peeing in the backyard, shouting "underwear" in the middle of a crowded store, or giving siblings haircuts?

Only you know your own children and what works and doesn't work with each of them. I think the best place to get advice regarding raising your children is from other parents. You can take the advice and ideas offered by those who have been-there-done-that and apply it in a way that works for your kids. Taking video games away from my middle son would be an effective way to get him to clean his room. The same punishment for my middle daughter would do absolutely nothing. I could ban my oldest daughter from using the phone and she'd think her life was ending. Those same consequences would have no effect on my oldest son. I'd only have to tell my middle daughter to do something, and she'd do it. To get compliance from my youngest son, I'd probably have to bribe him with candy (hey, I never said I was perfect).

Other parents are the only ones who can truly understand what you mean when you say, "They look like angels. When they're sleeping." Other parents know where you're coming from when you say you're so frustrated with the kids that you want to run away. They can also relate when you cover those little darlings' faces with kisses and say that you could just eat them up. Any other parent knows what it's like to beam with pride over a child's wonderful report card or at something nice he just did for a relative or when she keeps her room clean for more than two hours. Parents all over can sympathize with your torn emotions when your child, wearing new sneakers, jumps in a mud puddle and then smiles up at you and explains "it was so much fun." Or when that child writes "I love Mommy" on the kitchen table in permanent marker or destroys the kitchen while making you a surprise breakfast in bed consisting of melted ice cream, cereal, and tomatoes.

This is what parenting's about. It's not about having a clean house or cooking five-star meals. It's not about volunteering for every position that arises. It's not about being the perfect parent. And it's not about controlling your kids.

It's about teaching your kids. It's about giving your children choices and enforcing the consequences that come with each choice. It's about spending time with your children and appreciating all their wonderful, unique qualities. It's not about trying to stop the crazy stuff that happens every day, but instead, it's about finding the fun and humor in the crazy stuff. It's about seeing the world through a child's eyes again. And mostly, it's about loving your children and making sure they know it.

Enjoy this time. Even when they make you crazy, these are the best days of your life.

A Conversation with Dawn Meehan

You say that the wild success of your eBay auctions was "God's way of telling [you] to share [your] stories," to use your talents to "encourage parents everywhere." How do you think your life would be different right now if you had not started blogging?

Well, for one thing, my kids wouldn't ask, "Are you going to blog about this?" every time they made a mess or got into something. And I'd have a lot more time on my hands. But I'd be missing out on the interaction with my readers (predominantly moms who are experiencing the same trials and tribulations that I am).

You write about how your kids have been the best teachers when it comes to parenting. What do you think is the most important thing they've taught you about parenting? What has been the most surprising lesson?

The most important thing my kids have taught me is that a parent needs a sense of humor. Parents need to able to laugh at the little things.

I've learned all sorts of surprising lessons! I've learned that blue Popsicles turn kids' poop neon green, that Barbies don't flush well, and that it's not a good idea to put yogurt in the lawn-mower's gas tank.

You say that there are a lot of parenting skills that aren't covered in books. What were you most unprepared for with your first baby?
I think the lack of sleep hit me the hardest. There's just no way to fully prepare yourself for that.

How were things different with each child?
I have definitely become more relaxed more with each addition to my family. With experience comes a certain level of comfort. While I freaked out when my first child got a cold or hurt himself or was resistant to potty training, I knew that these things were not the end of the world with my subsequent children.

Do you think you became a better parent as you went along?
Absolutely. I joke that my first couple of kids were my experimental kids. Then I got good at this whole parenting thing. Of course, by the time the sixth one came around, I think I just got tired and worn out, which would explain why I don't care if she eats nothing but M&Ms and ketchup for a week.

I've learned to really enjoy my time with my kids because it flies by so quickly. And I've learned to not sweat the small stuff. When kids color on the walls, give their little sisters a haircut, or break a window playing ball, it's not a big deal. It's small potatoes in the whole scheme of things. Life is so much more pleasant when you don't dwell on those little things and instead find a balance in teaching children to be responsible adults while still letting them be kids.

As your children get older, is there anything you wish you had done differently? Do you think having regrets comes with being a parent?
I remember briefly wishing I hadn't taught my toddler how to

walk because walking is highly overrated; it opens whole new worlds of mischief for kids. Honestly, this isn't something I dwell on. You can't turn back time and change anything, so why worry about what you might have done differently? I think even mistakes have their place. You learn from them and you move on. Somehow the things you might wish you'd done a little differently have a way of turning out just fine in the end.

It seems like some of the best coping mechanisms you've found for dealing with the everyday struggles of being a single mom (and parenting in general!) are your close friendships and your sense of humor. How have these both helped you along the way? Why is a good sense of humor so important?

You have a choice at how you view your circumstances. You can be mad and bitter and think, Why did this happen to me? Or you can look at it in a positive light. You can find the humor (and there's always humor to be found!) and laugh at the funny parts while maintaining the belief that God will take care of you and that this too shall pass (and it always does).

And my friends are invaluable! When I start to get overwhelmed, they're there to pick me up and remind me that I'm loved. Whether they share some inspiring scripture with me, offer to pick up my kids from school, listen to me whine for a bit, or offer to take me out for the other kind of wine, they're the best!

We put a lot of pressure on our kids today to be star athletes, play an instrument, do volunteer work, go to church, get good grades, and spend time with their family and friends. Do you think kids are overprogrammed? Have you ever considered cutting back some of the afterschool activities?

I think a lot of kids are overwhelmed with activities. Because my finances are limited and I have six kids and haven't developed a cloning device yet, my children are limited to one activity each.

They get to participate in activities they like, yet they still have time to play and just be kids.

We also put a lot of pressure on moms today to do it all! How do you deal with this pressure? Do you feel like you have enough time to take care of yourself and be the kind of mom that you want to be? **I definitely don't feel like I can do it all and I admit that taking care of myself is last on my list. But unlike a lot of moms, I'm okay with that. I really don't feel like I'm losing out. I feel like my kids are my priority right now. That's why I had them. If I wanted to have tons of time to care for myself, I wouldn't have had children. In a way, caring for them is caring for myself because it makes me feel good to nurture my children. The day will come (and sooner than I'd like, I'm sure) where I'll have so much time for myself, I won't know what to do with it all!**

You mention how your mom created special family traditions for you and your sister, such as shopping for Easter outfits or decorating the Christmas tree the day after Thanksgiving. What family traditions do you want to create for your kids? What new traditions have you started with your family since you've been a single mom?
I've created all sorts of fun traditions! Traditions like Mom Doesn't Feel Like Cooking so We're Having Frozen Pizza Fridays, Late to School Mondays, and Everybody Pitches in to Get the House Clean Saturdays so Mom Doesn't Throw a Fit Because She Has to Do It Herself have become regular occurrences in my house.

A few years ago I bought a journal, and every Christmas we pass it around to all the family members so they can record their thoughts about the day: what they're thankful for, who celebrated Christmas with us, a favorite present they gave or received, what we had for dinner, what the weather was like, and so forth. We enjoy looking back through all the entries each year. We've also started the tradition of going around the table at dinner so each person can take a turn talking about the best and worst things that happened during their day. We've started spending more time together as a family (not that we didn't before), but now that I'm a single mom and their father isn't in the picture, I feel it's even more important to connect as a family and be there for each other.

Might not other parents read about some of your family's antics and react negatively to your parenting style?
Nah. I just tell myself that clearly other parents react negatively because they're just jealous of my stellar parenting skills; after all, I'm always right and they're wrong. Seriously, I don't do things to impress other people and don't care much what they think. There isn't one correct way to parent; you do what works for your family. Just because your way is different from someone else's doesn't make it wrong. Being a mom of so many kids has taught me that children are all different and what works for one may not work for another. You just can't judge how other parents raise their children because you're not in their shoes.

Do you personally feel like you've been a successful parent?
Define successful.

What's up next for you and your family?
We're starting a brand-new adventure! We're moving from Chicago to Orlando this summer. From what I understand, we'll be experiencing heat and humidity, bugs the size of Buicks, and hurricanes. We're looking forward to it!

Also available from

DAWN MEEHAN

"Her funny and unvarnished tales of the daily drudgeries of motherhood have made her the author of an incredibly popular Mommy blog."

—*ABC World News*

HOWARD BOOKS
A Division of Simon & Schuster
A CBS COMPANY

Printed in the United States
By Bookmasters